I0569204

Catalogue of permanent circulation coin and paper money types

Volume I

The Netherlands

Catalogue of permanent circulation coin and paper money types.
Volume I. The Netherlands

by H G M Eggenkamp-Vlaanderen

©2016, Dr HGM Eggenkamp-Vlaanderen

ISBN 978-90-816059-7-7 (Soft cover)

Onderzoek & Beleving, Bussum, The Netherlands

post@onderzoek-en-beleving.nl

Catalogue of permanent circulation coin and paper money types

Volume I

The Netherlands

H. G. M. Eggenkamp-Vlaanderen

1st edition, 2016

Preface

The period of modern numismatics (since about 1800) is perhaps the most interesting ever. Within this period different types of standards (silver, gold, bimetallic) alternated, and periods of sometimes impressive inflation occurred, in many countries even resulting in hyperinflation. The period after World War II even is the first period in the Earth's history that continued inflation is the norm. It also is the period that paper money took over as the main appearance of currency money. This started towards the end of the 19th century when gold coins were mostly stored in vaults and money circulated primarily in the form of banknotes. This became especially important during World Wars I and II when silver and gold coins were hoarded and were replaced by different kinds of paper money in circulation. After World War II no longer circulation gold coins were issued anymore and in most countries even silver coins disappeared from circulation in the years after World War II. As a result at this moment coins are solely "small change" in most countries while paper money is used for larger payments. Of course only when payment is made in currency and not taking into account the plastic and even "telephone" money that is increasingly becoming more important. In most countries the trend is that more and more of the payments are done by electronic means, so the importance of currency for payment has decreased and is expected to continue to decrease considerably in the near future.

In this series of books the different appearances of currency money (both coins and different types of paper and polymer money) are classified into one system. The reason is that the author believes that it is necessary to look at both appearances to understand the circulation of money in a society. In most current catalogues coins and paper money are treated separate and in many cases it is even necessary to acquire different catalogues for coins and for paper money. In fact, the collection of coins and the collection of paper money are very often considered as different fields of collection and study and most people either collect coins or collect paper money but not both. However, during the lifetime to a certain denomination coins and paper money series can alternate. For example, in the Netherlands the silver Gulden coin disappeared from circulation in 1914 at the start of World War I, and was replaced by a paper silver certificate with the same value. After the war was over and the situation normalised these paper certificates could be withdrawn. The same happened during World War II (1940-1945), when silver Gulden coins disappeared again, only to be returned to circulation, although in a smaller version, almost 10 years after the war ended. In other words, to understand the circulation in a country, it is necessary to understand how coins and paper money did alternate in history.

What I consider a problem for the collector of circulation coins (and increasingly also for paper money) is the increased issue of all kind of commemorative coins (and notes). Especially after about 1980 the number of commemorative coins has increased in many countries to such an extend that the regular circulations coins, the coins that the public on the street actually uses in commerce, are hardly visible in the major catalogues anymore. This is one of the main reasons that this catalogues has been prepared and the main reason that only very little information on commemorative coins is provided. They are mentioned if they comply to circulation specification and if they are issued in relatively large quantities at face value. But without images which are provided solely for the regular permanent types.

The currency described in this series is classified according to a newly developed classification scheme. This scheme is built as a hierarchical system based on i) the nominal value, ii) the year a new coin or note series is issued for the first time, iii) the year of issue and iv) if more than one varieties are issued per year an indication for these varieties. In the case of a redenomination or a monetary reform takes place the new currency unit is fit into the old one. For example, the old Franc in France has been replaced by the new Franc, at a ration of 100:1, in 1959. As the nominal value in the classification does not change the new Franc will get the same nominal value at the first hierarchical level as the old 100 Franc. This way it is hoped that historical continuity is shown clearly in the series presented in these catalogues.

This series of catalogues has been prepared with mainly one collector/numismatist in mind, notably myself. I was already looking for the "ideal" catalogue for a while, and in my opinion it seemed that this was not available. For that reason I decided that I should prepare this catalogue myself. This book series, of which this is the first volume and of which more will be produced in the near future, is the result of this endeavour.

I would like to thank "De Nederlandsche Bank" and the "European Central Bank" for their clear explanation how images of bank notes can be used in a publication like this. The ECB is thanked for making available images of the Euro banknotes on their website. Most importantly I would like to thank my wife, Nina Vlaanderen-Eggenkamp, for her support during the production of this book.

It is hoped that this series of type catalogues will fill the gap that exists for people that are mostly (or even only) interested in circulation coins, or people that want to learn about the combined history of the currency, both in metal or paper form. They will get an overview of actually used currency in a country, and get a (good) impression of the money that really circulated between the people.

Hans Eggenkamp-Vlaanderen

Introduction to the series

Each volume in this series describes the circulating currency, defined as the coins and paper money that circulate, in a certain, more or less defined area, in most volumes a single country. Although this may seem vague, the reason is that it is aimed to classify the circulating money in a way that shows the continuity of the money in a region over a longer time span, mostly from the early 19th century until the present day. In several countries significant political changes have happened during this long period, and this is generally reflected in the money that circulated in the specific country. Well known examples are countries that were colonised during the 19th century and became independent during the 20th, as well as countries that were occupied by another country for longer or shorter periods during the last two centuries. Also mergers and split-ups of countries are reflected in the circulating currency. An example of colonisation and subsequent independence will be Indonesia, where the coins and notes of the Dutch East Indies will be incorporated as this was the name of Indonesia before its independence. More complex histories are shown in the cases of central Europe (for example Austria-Hungary and its successor states) where significant territorial changes have occurred after World War I (in 1918) and during World War II (1939-1945) as well as after the collapse of communist eastern Europe in 1990. Other examples are the former Yugoslavia and Russia/the former Soviet Union.

Apart from this there are several differences between the major well known catalogues and this catalogue series. It is not a prize catalogue. So no indications are given concerning the collector values of the coins or banknotes. I believe there is no real need to supply values as these are easily findable on various specialised internet sites such as Ebay.com, Catawiki.com and Numista.com. And these values are by definition more up to date than values in a printed catalogue. For the same reason no attempt have been made to discuss the grade of the coins and paper money types. The images presented in this catalogue are not necessary of high quality specimens and sometimes they even are of specimens of only the quality "good". The reason is that they are taken form my personal collection that not always consists of better quality specimens.

The catalogue aims to present a *what I would call a* "scientific" classification of the coins and paper money series and types, including a "scientific" way of giving references for each series and type. Although I tried to add images for as many as possible coins and paper money types (that is the "permanent" types only) not all have been pictures. The reason is that I do not have pictures of all permanent types available. Most coins are images from specimens present in my personal collection. 19th century line drawings are taken from contemporary books mostly available from Google books. Bank notes are either scans from my personal collection or obtained from websites from Central Banks after consultation with the relevant division. In some cases even images were made available by the issuing bank. No commemorative coins and banknotes are pictured in this series of catalogues. As written before one of the main reasons for writing this catalogue series is the fact that commemoratives are taking too much space in many modern catalogues and are making the regular circulating coins and notes more and more invisible. Some commemorative series are mentioned however, if the issue limits are relatyively large and if they are issued at face value, so that at least a small chance existed that they were used in commerce. However, no images of these coins are supplied. As this catalogue is a "type only" catalogue the individual mintage years for coins and years, dates and signature combinations for paper money are also not mentioned.

Table of Contents

xi

The Netherlands

The Netherlands is a constitutional monarchy in Northwestern Europe. The country has a surface (land) area of 41,543 km^2 and a population of 16,947,904.

Location of The Netherlands within Europe (CIA The World Factbook)

Map of The Netherlands showing the main cities (CIA The World Factbook)

In this catalogue the coins that are issued since 1817 and paper money (banknotes) that are issued since 1814 are described. In 1814 the national bank ("De Nederlandsche Bank") was formed. This institute has, until the introduction of the Euro in 2002, always been the only institute with the right to issue bank notes in the Netherlands. The national currency, the Gulden, was decimalised in 1817, and for that reason that year has been chosen as starting point for the incorporation of coins.

What coins and notes are incorporated in this catalogue? Circulating coin series issued at face value since 1817, all banknotes issued by "De Nederlandsche Bank" between 1814 and 2001 and the European Central Bank since 2002 and treasury notes and silver certificates issued by the ministry of finances of the Netherlands. This includes the commemorative coins issued at face value in relatively large quantities, which however are not pictured in this catalogue. This indicates that coin series solely consisting of commemorative coins only have an indication of type and size and the period they were issued. Not incorporated are commemorative coin series issued above face value only in small mintages (such as the recent gold 10, 20 and 50 Euro coins), and trade coins without the status of legal tender (gold and silver ducats), except when these trade coins have the same specifications as legal value coins that they replaced.

In the period 1814/1817 until 2015 the Netherlands used two currency units. Until 2001 this was the Gulden, since 1999 the Euro. The period between 1999 and 2001 was a period that the two currencies overlapped. During this period the circulating currency still was the Gulden, while Euros only existed as money of account although coins were already minted from 1999. These were held in storage until they were distributed to the public towards the end of 2001. The exchange from Gulden to Euro was a redenomination, with 1 Euro equal to 2.20371 Gulden.

In this catalogue only coins and banknotes that were issued (in principle) in the whole country are classified. These are the coins issued by the treasury which have the head or the monogram of the reigning monarch on them, or just a plain legend, either "NEDERLAND" or "KONINGRIJK DER NEDERLANDEN". In only one instance, one of the two 1 cent coins issued in 1901, as legend "KONINKRIJK DER NEDERLANDEN" was used, thus with a "K" in stead of a "G" in the first word. Although the word "koninkrijk" might be the proper spelling of the Dutch word for "kingdom" in the law it was specified that it should be "koningrijk" and for that reason it continued so until the last minted coins from Queen Wilhelmina in 1945. The following kings and queens have reigned the Netherlands: Willem I (coins issued between

1817 and 1840), Willem II (issue dates 1840-1849), Willem III (issue dates 1849-1890), Wilhelmina (issue dates 1891-1948), Juliana (issue dates 1950-1980), Beatrix (issue dates 1980-2013) and Willem-Alexander (issue dates since 2013). Paper money that is classified in this catalogue is issued by the treasury (silver certificates and treasury notes), De Nederlandsche Bank (banknotes in Gulden until 2001, last dated note 1997) and the European Central Bank (banknotes in Euro since 2002).

Classification system

The classification developed for this book series uses a hierarchical system as described below.

i) The first level is based on the logarithm (base 10) of the nominal values of the coins and paper money that is issued in the country. This is determined by taking the logarithm of the nominal value, add the lowest number to get a positive result, multiply by 10 and put a "O" before. For example the lowest denomination in the Netherlands is the half cent (NLG 0.005), the logarithm is -2.3, to make it positive 3 is added (so that the result is 0.7) then it is multiplied by 10 (so as to get 7) then a leading 0 (zero) and an "O" is added in front and a slash at the end (so that the general code for "half cent" is "O07/"). In this system the Gulden gets the code "O30/". A redenomination will not change the value. So, 1 Euro (2,20 Gulden) is "O33/", and the logarithmic value of 10 cents (NLG 0.10) is equal to that of the 5 eurocent (EUR 0.05), both "O20/".

ii) The second level indicates the actual coin or note series. A coin series is a series of coins issued according to a defined nominal value and well defined technical specifications that include (at least) metal composition, coin shape, weight and diameter. Note series are defined less strict but mostly by the nominal value, the design (a small change indicates a note within the same series, a completely new design defines a new note series) the size and the composition of the note. The series are defined (classified) by the first year that a coin or note series is either minted, authorised or issued. It depends on the information that is readily available. For coin series it is the year that is normally accepted as the first year a coin is officially minted. This is the year that in most catalogues is accepted as the first year of mintage. This is not necessary a year with a high mintage. For note series this is the year that the note is authorised, and that is printed on the note. This year is in most cases one to three years before the note is actually issued in the Netherlands. After the year either a "C" or an "N" is added to indicate if the series is a coin or a note series. In those cases that more than one series was issued or authorised in the same year a superscript "1" or "2" etc. is added.

iii) The third level indicates the year that an individual coin or note is minted or issued as indicated on the note or coin. For coins this is the mintage year as indicated on the coin. For notes the system is necessarily more complicated. On notes issued in the Netherlands different combinations of dates and signatures are used. Early bank notes were signed and dated when issued, so that the year of issue is known. Normally they are however catalogued with the signature (combination in case more than one signature is present) and a different catalogue indication is given when a signature changes. Modern banknotes and older treasury notes have a fixed date/signature combination so that there is not need to add a third level classification. Bank notes issued by the European Central Bank contain the year that a bank note is issued and the signature of the current President of the Bank. The year at this level for these notes indicates the first year that a given President has taken office.

iv) At the final level the variability within a coin or note series is indicated. For standard circulation coins this exists of a capital letter for the common obverse and reverse sides. A big change in the design is indicated by a different letter, small variations in the design by a superscript number. Different issues of the same obverse/reverse combinations in a year (such as the change of mintmaster's sign or coins minted at different mints) are indicated by small letters after the design indications. Commemorative coins are indicated with a "Z" at this level. When more commemoratives are issued in one year followed by a superscript number. If either the obverse of the reverse of a commemorative coin is of a standard design this is indicated at this level too, as for example will be used in modern 2 Euro commemorative coins. In this catalogue however no commemorative designs are described as it is a "permanent types" catalogue.

Set-up of the catalogue

In the following pages the coins and paper money series that circulated in the Netherlands are presented. Starting from the lowest nominal value (the half (Gulden) cent) until the highest nominal value (the 500 Euro banknote). Within each nominal value a short summary is given of the series (either coins or notes) that were issued and an indication is given of the periods that a certain nominal value was circulating in the country. After this introduction a table is presented that shows the various coin and note series, including the years these were issued, the composition, the mass, the diameter (size) and the thickness (THK) of the specimens in each series. The composition of the coin series is given as their metallic composition with percentages of the chemical elements. Here Cu is copper, Sn is tin, Zn is zinc, Ni is nickel, Ag is silver and Au is gold. When the thickness is given in available literature this is used, if it is not it is calculated from the size, weight and the metal composition of the coin. In the case of paper money series only the size (height x width) is given. No attempts are made to indicate the weight of the thickness of the paper money series. These tables give good impressions how coins and paper money series alternated for each nominal value.

Then a section is written for each coin or paper money series. For each coin series after the title a figure is available that shows the exact size of the coin. As paper money normally has a size that is larger than the size of a page in this book for paper money this is not given. This figure is followed by images and short descriptions of the obverse and reverse types. All coins are depicted at the same size of 1 inch or 2.54 cm, all paper money is depicted at a width of 1.8 inch or 4.57 cm, while the height if the paper money images depend on the actual width to height ratio of the note. Finally a table is presented that indicates the various coin or paper money types (possible obverse-reverse combinations) and the years that these combinations were issued. In the case of coins cross references are given with the major world coin catalogues (KM#, Standard Catalog of World Coins by CL Krause and C Mischler; S# Weltmunzkatalog 19. Jahrhundert by G Schön und H Kahn, and 20. und 21. Jahrhundert by G Schön und G. Schön and Y# A Catalog of Modern World Coins 1850-1964 by RS Yeoman). In the case of paper money a cross reference is given as the P# from the Standard Catalog of World Paper Money, either the 3rd edition by Albert Poick or the 9th edition by N Shafer and GS Cuhaj. Finally an empty column with "X" in the title is present in which the owner can indicate whether a specimen of the coin or paper money type is present in his or her own collection. The presence of commemorative coins in the coin series is roughly mentioned with the years they were issued, but no further descriptions are given.

The catalogue

1. O07/ Half cent (NLG 0.005)

Minted from 1818 until 1940, after which it was removed from circulation due to inflation. Issued as coins of two different types, one in copper (1818-1877) and one in bronze (1878-1940).

Type	Years	Comp.	Mass (g)	Size (mm)	THK (mm)
O07/1818C	1818-1877	Copper (100% Cu)	1.922	16	1.1
O07/1878C	1878-1940	Bronze (95% Cu, 4% Sn, 1% Zn)	1.25	14	0.9

1.1. O07/1818C Copper half cent (1818-1877)

One permanent obverse design and one permanent reverse design.

Obverse   *Reverse*

Obverse: Crowned "W" between year of mintage.

Reverse: NL coat of arms between "½" and "C.".

Subtype	Years	KM#	S#	Y#	X
O07/1818Cyyyy	1818-1877	51, 68, 90	25, 38, 48	1	

1.2. O07/1878C Bronze half cent (1878-1940)

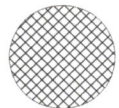

Two permanent obverse designs, the second of which has two subtypes. Two reverse designs of which the first has two subtypes.

Obverse A

Obverse B¹

Obverse B²

Obverse A: Heraldic lion in field with legend around.

Obverse B¹: As obverse A with modernised lion.

Obverse B²: As obverse B¹ with coarser lining on field.

Reverse A¹

Reverse A²

Reverse B

Reverse A¹: "½ CENT" within orange wreath.

Reverse A²: As reverse A¹ with wider nominal value.

Reverse B: As reverse A¹ with heavily redesigned wreath.

Subtype	Years	KM#	S#	Y#	X
O07/1878CyyyyAA[1]	1878-1901	109	50, 65 (19th cent.); 2 (20th cent.)	3	
O07/1878CyyyyB[1]A[2]	1903-1906	133	14	3	
O07/1878CyyyyB[2]B	1909-1940	138	30	35	

2. O10/ Cent (NLG 0.01)

Minted from 1817 until 1980, after which it was removed from circulation due to inflation. Issued as coins of four different types. Copper (1817-1877), large bronze (1877-1941), zinc (1941-1944) and small bronze (1948-1980).

Type	Years	Comp.	Mass (g)	Size (mm)	THK (mm)
O10/1817C	1818-1877	Copper (100% Cu)	3.845	22	1.1
O10/1877C	1877-1941	Bronze (95% Cu, 4% Sn, 1% Zn)	2.5	19	1.0
O10/1941C	1941-1944	Zinc (100% Zn)	2.0	17	1.2
O10/1948C	1948-1980	Bronze (95% Cu, 4% Sn, 1% Zn)	2.0	17	1.0

2.1. O10/1817C Copper cent (1817-1877)

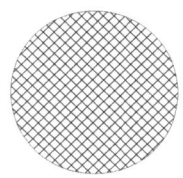

Issued with one obverse and one reverse design. The design was not changed when a new king ascended to the throne.

Obverse   *Reverse*

Obverse: Crowned W between year of mintage.

Reverse: NL coat of arms between "1" and "C.".

Subtype	Years	KM#	S#	Y#	X
O10/1817Cyyyy	1817-1877	47, 100	26, 49	2	

2.2. O10/1877C Large bronze cent (1877-1941)

Four permanent obverse designs, of which the last two have two subtypes. Two reverse designs of which the first has two subtypes. No commemorative issues.

Obverse A   *Obverse B*   *Obverse C¹*

10

Obverse C ²　　　　　*Obverse D¹*　　　　　*Obverse D²*

Obverse A: Heraldic lion in field with 15 small blocks and legend around.

Obverse B: Heraldic lion in field with 10 large blocks and legend around.

Obverse C¹: Redesigned heraldic lion in field with blocks. Legend reads "KONINKRIJK".

Obverse C²: Like obverse C¹ but legend reads "KONINGRIJK"

Obverse D¹: Redesigned heraldic lion (different crown) with very thick letters in legend.

Obverse D²: As obverse D¹ with thinner lettering in legend.

Reverse A¹　　　　　*Reverse A²*　　　　　*Reverse B*

Reverse A¹: "1 CENT" within orange wreath.

Reverse A²: As reverse A¹ with thinner "1" in nominal value.

Reverse B: As reverse A¹ with heavily redesigned wreath.

Subtype	Years	KM#	S#	Y#	X
O10/1877CyyyyAA¹	1877-1900	107	51, 66 (19th	4	

Subtype	Years	KM#	S#	Y#	X
			cent.), 3 (20th cent.)		
O10/1877CyyyyBA¹	1901	130	3	4	
O10/1877CyyyyC¹A²	1901	131	3	4	
O10/1877CyyyyC²A²	1902-1907	132	15	4	
O10/1877CyyyyD¹B	1913-1916	152	31	36	
O10/1877CyyyyD²B	1916-1941	152	31	36	

2.3. O10/1941C Zinc cent(1941-1944)

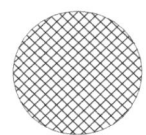

Issued during the occupation of the Netherlands during World War II, with with one obverse and one reverse design.

Obverse　　　　*Reverse*

Obverse: Cross with "NEDERLAND" on band.

Reverse: Value with waves and wheat ears.

Subtype	Years	KM#	S#	Y#	X
O10/1941Cyyyy	1941-1944	170	55	48	

2.4. O10/1948C Small bronze cent (1948-1980)

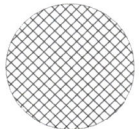

Two obverse and only one reverse designs were used for this coin type.

Obverse A   *Obverse B*   *Reverse A*

Obverse A: Head of Queen Wilhelmina facing left.

Obverse B: Head of Queen Juliana facing right.

Reverse A: Large 1 above "CENT".

Subtype	Years	KM#	S#	Y#	X
O10/1948CyyyyAA	1948	175	60	53	
O10/1877CyyyyBA[1]	1950-1980	130	64	57	

3. O13/ Eurocent (EUR 0.01)

Produced since 1999, in circulation since 2002 after the introduction of the Euro as the new European currency. Only one coin series has been produced since the introduction.

Series	Years	Comp.	Mass (g)	Size (mm)	THK (mm)
O13/1999C	1999-....	Copper plated steel (94.35% Fe with 5.65% Cu plating)	2.3	16.25	1.67

3.1. O13/1999C Copper plated steel eurocent (1999-....)

Two obverse types and one reverse type are issued until 2015. This coin is not used for commemorative issues. Although this coin is still minted in small quantities for collectors and is still officially legal tender it is no longer used in daily commerce since 2004. Due to the low purchasing value of the 1 and 2 eurocent coins prizes in the Netherlands are currently rounded to the nearest 5 eurocent.

Obverse A   *Obverse B*   *Reverse A*

Obverse A: Head of Queen Beatrix facing left.

Obverse B: Head of King Willem-Alexander facing right.

Reverse A: Value with a globe showing location of Europe.

Type	Years	KM#	S#	Y#	X
O13/1999CyyyyAA	1999-2013	234	117		
O13/1999CyyyyBA	2014-....				

4. O14/ 2½ cent (NLG 0.025)

Minted from 1877 until 1942. Removed from circulation (in 1948) when also the ½ cent was abolished, as it was no longer convenient change. Two series of 2½ cent coins have circulated, a bronze and a zinc.

Series	Years	Comp.	Mass (g)	Size (mm)	THK (mm)
O14/1877C	1877-1941	Bronze (95% Cu, 4% Sn, 1% Zn)	4.0	23.5	1.0
O14/1941C	1941-1942	Zinc (100% Zn)	2.8	20.0	1.3

4.1. O14/1877C Bronze 2½ cent (1877-1941)

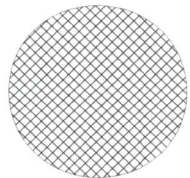

Three obverse and two reverse designs, the first of which has two subtypes. No commemorative issues.

Obverse A   *Obverse B*   *Obverse C*

Obverse A: Heraldic lion in field with 17 small blocks and legend around.

Obverse B: Heraldic lion in field with 15 larger blocks and legend around.

Obverse C: As reverses A and B with smaller crown and larger lettering of the legend.

Reverse A¹ *Reverse A²* *Reverse B*

Reverse A[1]: "2½ CENT" within orange wreath.

Reverse A[2]: As reverse A[1] with slightly redesigned wreath.

Reverse B: As reverse A with heavily redesigned wreath.

Type	Years	KM#	S#	Y#	X
O14/1877CyyyyAA¹	1877-1898	108	52, 67 (19th cent.), 4 (20th cent.)	5	
O14/1877CyyyyBA²	1903-1906	134	16	5	
O14/1877CyyyyCB	1912-1941	150	32	37	

4.2. O14/1941C Zinc 2½ cent (1941-1942)

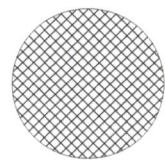

Minted in 1941 and 1942 although the latter in small numbers only almost all of which were remelted. Only one design.

Obverse *Reverse*

Obverse: Typical Frisian farmhouse façade decoration.

Reverse: As O10/1941C with "2½ ct".

Type	Years	KM#	S#	Y#	X
O14/1941Cyyyy	1941-1942	171	56	49	

5. O16/ 2 eurocent (EUR 0.02)

Produced since 1999, in circulation since 2002 after the introduction of the Euro as the new European currency. Only one coin series has been produced since the introduction.

Series	Years	Comp.	Mass (g)	Size (mm)	THK (mm)
O16/1999C	1999-....	Copper plated steel (94.35% Fe with 5.65% Cu plating)	3.0	18.75	1.67

5.1. O16/1999C Copper plated steel 2 eurocent (1999-....)

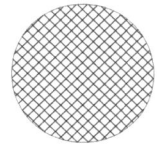

Two obverse types and one reverse type are issued until 2015. This coin is not used for commemorative issues. Although this coin is still minted in small quantities for collectors and is still officially legal tender it is no longer used in daily commerce since 2004. Due to the low purchasing value of the 1 and 2 eurocent coins prizes in the Netherlands are currently rounded to the nearest 5 eurocent.

| Obverse A | Obverse B | Reverse A |

Obverse A: Head of Queen Beatrix facing left.

Obverse B: Head of King Willem-Alexander facing right.

Reverse A: Value with a globe showing location of Europe.

Type	Years	KM#	S#	Y#	X
O16/1999CyyyyAA	1999-2013	235	118		
O161999CyyyyBA	2014-....				

6. O17/ 5 cent (NLG 0.05)

Issued as coins during the whole period the Gulden was the currency of the Netherlands. Removed from circulation in 2002 after the introduction of the Euro. A total of six coin series were issued during this period. None of them contained commemorative issues.

Series	Years	Comp.	Mass (g)	Size (mm)	THK (mm)
O17/1818C	1818-1828	Silver (56.9% Ag, 43.1% Cu)	0.846	15.0	0.4
O17/1848C	1848-1887	Silver (64% Ag, 36% Cu)	0.685	12.5	0.5
O17/1907C	1907-1909	Copper-nickel (75% Cu, 25% Ni)	4.50	18.0	2.1
O17/1913C	1913-1940	Copper-nickel (75% Cu, 25% Ni)	4.50	square, 18x18	1.5
O17/1941C	1941-1943	Zinc (100% Zn)	3.60	square, 18x18	1.6
O17/1948	1948-2001	Bronze (95%	3.50	21.0	1.4

Series	Years	Comp.	Mass (g)	Size (mm)	THK (mm)
		Cu, 4% Sn, 1% Zn)			

6.1. O17/1818C Large silver 5 cents (1818-1828)

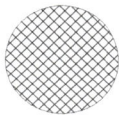

Issued with one obverse and one reverse design.

Obverse   *Reverse*

Obverse: Mintage year divided by crowned "W".

Reverse: NL coat of arms between "5" and "C.".

Type	Years	KM#	S#	Y#	X
O17/1818Cyyyy	1818-1828	52	27		

6.2. O17/1848C Small silver 5 cents (1848-1887)

Issued with two obverse and one reverse designs. However, as the dies of Obverse A were only ready after the King was deceased only a small number were minted for testing purposes.

Obverse B   *Reverse A*

Obverse A: Head of King Willem II facing left.

Obverse B: Head of King Willem III facing right.

Reverse A: "5 CENTS" within wreath of oak leaves.

Type	Years	KM#	S#	Y#	X
O17/1848CyyyyAA	1848	74	39		
O17/1848CyyyyBA	1850-1887	91	53	6	

6.3. O17/1907C Round copper-nickel 5 cents (1907-1909)

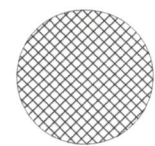

Issued for only three years due to confusion with equally sized 25 cent coin. Only one obverse and one reverse design.

Obverse   *Reverse*

Obverse: Royal crown between two oak leaves.

Reverse: "5 CENTS" between two orange leaves.

Type	Years	KM#	S#	Y#	X
O17/1907Cyyyy	1907-1909	137	17	33	

6.4. O17/1913C Square copper-nickel 5 cents (1913-1940)

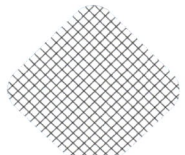

With the same weight as the last, a square coin would no longer be confused with the 25 cents coin. Only one obverse and one reverse design.

Obverse   *Reverse*

Obverse: Legend between two circles with orange leaf inside.

Reverse: Value "5 c" in circle with shells at the edges.

Type	Years	KM#	S#	Y#	X
O17/1913Cyyyy	1913-1940	153	33	34	

6.5. O17/1941C Zinc 5 cents (1941-1943)

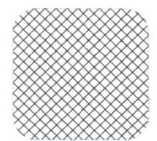

Issued during the occupation of the Netherlands during World War II, with with one obverse and one reverse design.

Obverse   *Reverse*

Obverse: Saxon horse heads (like 2½ cents façade decoration) with sun above.

Reverse: "5 c" in circle with waves at left and wheat ear at right.

Type	Years	KM#	S#	Y#	X
O17/1941Cyyyy	1941-1943	172	57	50	

6.6. O17/1948C Bronze 5 cent (1948-2001)

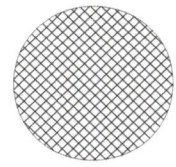

Three obverse and two reverse designs.

Obverse A   *Obverse B*   *Obverse C*

Obverse A: Head of Queen Wilhelmina facing left.

Obverse B: Head of Queen Juliana facing right.

Obverse C: Head of Queen Beatrix facing left.

Reverse A   *Reverse B*

Reverse A: "5 CENT" decorated with an orange leave.

Reverse B: "5 ct" on a grid representing the value.

Type	Years	KM#	S#	Y#	X
O17/1948CyyyyAA	1948	176	61	54	
O17/1948CyyyyBA	1950-1980	181	65	58	
O17/1948CyyyyCB	1982-2001	202	82		

7. O20/ 10 cent (NLG 0.10); 5 eurocent (EUR 0.05)

Because the nominal value of 5 eurocent is only 10% higher than 10 (gulden)cent they fall under the same heading as their nominal values are close enough to have the same logarithm after rounding. The 10 cent was last minted in 2001 and removed from circulation in 2002, the 5 eurocent was first minted in 1999 and appeared in circulation in 2002. Four series of 10 cent coins and one series of 5 eurocent coins have been produced.

Series	Years	Comp.	Mass (g)	Size (mm)	THK (mm)
O20/1818C	1818-1828	Silver (56.9% Ag, 43.1% Cu)	1.692	18.0	0.6
O20/1848C	1848-1945	Silver (64% Ag, 36% Cu)	1.40	15.0	1.0
O20/1941C	1941-1943	Zinc (100% Zn)	3.30	22.0	1.4
O20/1948C	1948-2001	Nickel (100% Ni)	1.50	15.0	1.2
O20/1999C	1999-....	Copper plated	3.90	21.25	1.67

Series	Years	Comp.	Mass (g)	Size (mm)	THK (mm)
		steel (94.35% Fe with 5.65% Cu plating)			

7.1. O20/1818C Large silver 10 cents (1818-1828)

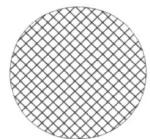

Issued with one obverse and one reverse design.

Obverse   *Reverse*

Obverse: Crowned. "W" between divided mintage year.

Reverse: NL coat of arms between "10" and "C.".

Type	Years	KM#	S#	Y#	X
O20/1818Cyyyy	1818-1828	53	28		

7.2. O20/1848C Small silver 10 cents (1848-1945)

During the long time that this coin series was issued a total of six obverse types, one of which with two subtypes and one with three subtypes, and two reverse types, the

24

first with two subtypes and the second with four subtypes, were issued.

Obverse A   Obverse B   Obverse C¹

Obverse C²   Obverse D²   Obverse D³

Obverse E   Obverse F

Obverse A: Head of King Willem II facing left.

Obverse B: Head of King Willem III facing right.

Obverse C¹:Head of Queen Wilhemina as a child with hair hanging down facing left.

Obverse C²: As obverse C¹ with slightly wider head.

Obverse D¹: Head of Queen Wilhelmina designed for her inauguration facing left.

Obverse D²: As obverse D¹ with slightly larger head.

Obverse D³: As obverse D¹ with legend extending un

der head.

Obverse E: Head of Queen Wilhelmina wearing ermine coat facing left.

Obverse F: Older head of Queen Wilhelmina facing left.

Reverse A¹   *Reverse A²*   *Reverse B¹*

Reverse B²   *Reverse B³*   *Reverse B⁴*

Reverse A¹: "10 CENTS" between two oak leaves.

Reverse A²: As reverse A¹ with slightly redesigned oak leaves.

Reverse B¹: As reverse A with considerably enlarged oak leaves and enlarged lettering.

Reverse B²: As reverse B¹ with slightly smaller oak leaves.

Reverse B³: As reverse B² with beads far from rim of coin.

Reverse B⁴: As reverse B³ with beads approaching rim.

Type	Years	KM#	S#	Y#	X
O20/1848CyyyyAA¹	1848-1849	75	40		
O20/1848CyyyyBA¹	1849-1890	80	54	7	
O20/1848CyyyyC¹A¹	1892	116	68	20	
O20/1848CyyyyC²A¹	1893-1897	116	68	20	

Type	Years	KM#	S#	Y#	X
O20/1848CyyyyD¹A¹	1898	119	5 (20th cen.)	23	
O20/1848CyyyyD¹A²	1901	119	5	23	
O20/1848CyyyyD²A²	1903	135	18	23a	
O20/1848CyyyyD³A²	1904-1906	136	19	23b	
O20/1848CyyyyEB¹	1910-1917	145	34	39	
O20/1848CyyyyEB²	1918-1925	145	34	39	
O20/1848CyyyyFB³	1926-1934	163	43	43	
O20/1848CyyyyFB⁴	1935-1945	163	43	43	

7.3. O20/1941C Zinc 10 cents (1941-1943)

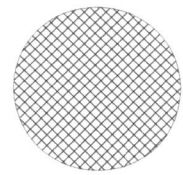

Issued during the occupation of the Netherlands during World War II, with with one obverse and one reverse design.

Obverse   *Reverse*

Obverse: Three stylised tulips.

Reverse: "10 CENTS" between two twigs.

Type	Years	KM#	S#	Y#	X
O20/1941Cyyyy	1941-1943	173	58	51	

7.4. O20/1948C Nickel 10 cent (1948-2001)

Three obverse and two reverse designs.

Obverse A   *Obverse B*   *Obverse C*

Obverse A: Head of Queen Wilhelmina facing left.

Obverse B: Head of Queen Juliana facing right.

Obverse C: Head of Queen Beatrix facing left.

Reverse A   *Reverse B*

Reverse A: Crowned "10 CENT".

Reverse B: "10 ct" on a grid representing the value.

Type	Years	KM#	S#	Y#	X
O20/1948CyyyyAA	1948	177	62	55	
O20/1948CyyyyBA	1950-1980	182	66	59	
O20/1948CyyyyCB	1982-2001	203	83		

7.5. O20/1999C Copper plated steel 5 eurocent (1999-....)

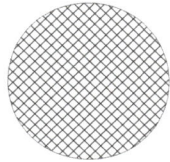

Two obverse types and one reverse type were issued until 2015.

Obverse A   *Obverse B*   *Reverse A*

Obverse A: Head of Queen Beatrix facing left.

Obverse B: Head of King Willem-Alexander facing right.

Reverse A: Value with a globe showing location of Europe.

Type	Years	KM#	S#	Y#	X
O20/1999CyyyyAA	1999-2013	236	119		
O20/1999CyyyyBA	2014-....				

8. O23/ 10 eurocent (EUR 0.10)

Produced since 1999, in circulation since 2002 after the introduction of the Euro as the new European currency. Only one coin series has been produced since the introduction.

Series	Years	Comp.	Mass (g)	Size (mm)	THK (mm)
O23/1999C	1999-....	Nordic gold (89% Cu, 5% Zn, 5% Al, 1% Sn)	4.10	19.75	1.93

8.1. O23/1999C Nordic gold 10 eurocent (1999-....)

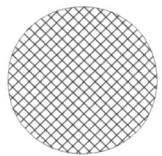

Two obverse types and two reverse types are issued until 2015.

Obverse A   *Obverse B*

Obverse A: Head of Queen Beatrix facing left.

Obverse B: Head of King Willem-Alexander facing right.

Reverse A   *Reverse B*

Reverse A: Value next to individually outlined European countries.

Reverse B: Value next to map of Europe.

Type	Years	KM#	S#	Y#	X
O23/1999CyyyyAA	1999-2006	237	120		
O23/1999CyyyyAB	2007-2013	268	152		
O23/1999CyyyyBB	2014-....				

9. O24/ 25 cent (NLG 0.25)

Issued as coins during the whole period that the Gulden was the currency of the Netherlands. Removed from circulation in 2002 after the introduction of the Euro. A total of four coin series were issued during this period. None of them contained commemorative issues.

Series	Years	Comp.	Mass (g)	Size (mm)	THK (mm)
O24/1817C	1817-1830	Silver (56.9% Ag, 43.1% Cu)	4.23	21	1.5
O24/1848C	1848-1945	Silver (64% Ag, 36% Cu)	3.575	19	1.5
O24/1941C	1941-1943	Zinc (100% Zn)	5.00	26	1.4
O24/1948C	1948-2001	Nickel (100% Ni)	3.00	19	1.5

9.1. O24/1817C Large silver 25 cents (1817-1830)

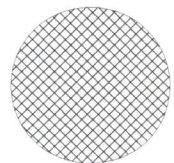

Issued with one obverse and one reverse design.

Obverse   *Reverse*

Obverse: Crowned W between year of mintage.

Reverse: NL coat of arms between 25 and C.

Type	Years	KM#	S#	Y#	X
O24/1817Cyyyy	1817-1830	48	29		

9.2. O24/1848C Small silver 25 cents (1848-1945)

During the long time that this coin series was issued a total of six obverse types, one of which with two subtypes, and two reverse types, the second of which with two subtypes, were issued.

Obverse A	*Obverse B*	*Obverse C*

Obverse D²	*Obverse E*	*Obverse F*

Obverse A: Head of King Willem II facing left.

Obverse B: Head of King Willem III facing right.

Obverse C: Head of Queen Wilhemina as a child with hair hanging down facing left.

Obverse D¹: Head of Queen Wilhelmina designed for her inauguration facing left.

Obverse D²: As obverse D² with narrower neck.

Obverse E: Head of Queen Wilhelmina wearing ermine coat facing left.

Obverse F: Older head of Queen Wilhelmina facing left.

Reverse A   *Reverse B¹*   *Reverse B²*

Reverse A: "25 CENTS" between two oak leaves.

Reverse B¹: As reverse A with considerably enlarged oak leaves and enlarged lettering.

Reverse B²: As reverse B¹, with slightly smaller oak leaves, visible from the larger distance between leaves and beads.

Type	Years	KM#	S#	Y#	X
O24/1848CyyyyAA	1848-1849	76	41		
O24/1848CyyyyBA	1849-1890	81	55	8	
O24/1848CyyyyCA	1891-1897	115	69	21	
O24/1848CyyyyD¹A	1898-1901	120.1	6 (20th cent.)	24	
O24/1848CyyyyD²A	1901-1906	120.2	20	24	
O24/1848CyyyyEB¹	1910-1925	146	35	40	
O24/1848CyyyyFB²	1926-1945	164	35	40	

9.3. O24/1941C Zinc 25 cents (1941-1943)

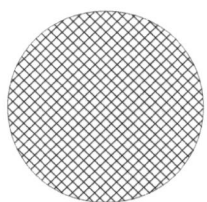

Issued during the occupation of the Netherlands during World War II, with with one obverse and one reverse design.

Obverse   *Reverse*

Obverse: Sailing ship.

Reverse: "25 CENTS" between two twigs.

Type	Years	KM#	S#	Y#	X
O24/1941Cyyyy	1941-1943	174	59	52	

9.4. O24/1948C Nickel 25 cent (1948-2001)

Three obverse and two reverse designs.

Obverse A   *Obverse B*   *Obverse C*

Obverse A: Head of Queen Wilhelmina facing left.

Obverse B: Head of Queen Juliana facing right.

Obverse C: Head of Queen Beatrix facing left.

Reverse A   *Reverse B*

Reverse A: Crowned "25 CENT".

Reverse B: "25 ct" on a grid representing the value.

Type	Years	KM#	S#	Y#	X
O24/1948CyyyyAA	1948	178	63	56	
O24/1948CyyyyBA	1950-1980	183	67	60	
O24/1948CyyyyCB	1982-2001	204	84		

10. O26/ 20 eurocent (EUR 0.20)

Produced since 1999, in circulation since 2002 after the introduction of the Euro as the new European currency. Only one coin series has been produced since the introduction.

Series	Years	Comp.	Mass (g)	Size (mm)	THK (mm)
O26/1999C	1999-....	Nordic gold (89% Cu, 5% Zn, 5% Al, 1% Sn)	5.70	22.25	2.14

10.1. O26/1999C Nordic gold 20 eurocent (1999-....)

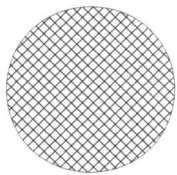

Two obverse types and two reverse types are issued until 2015.

Obverse A   *Obverse B*

Obverse A: Head of Queen Beatrix facing left.

Obverse B: Head of King Willem-Alexander facing right.

Reverse A   *Reverse B*

Reverse A: Value next to individually outlined European countries.

Reverse B: Value next to map of Europe.

Type	Years	KM#	S#	Y#	X
O26/1999CyyyyAA	1999-2006	238	121		
O26/1999CyyyyAB	2007-2013	269	153		
O26/1999CyyyyBB	2014-....				

11. O27/ ½ Gulden (NLG 0.50)

Issued between 1818 and 1930. This was never a very popular nominal value in the European part of the Netherlands and most of them were exported to Netherlands India. Three coin series were issued of this nomination.

Series	Years	Comp.	Mass (g)	Size (mm)	THK (mm)
O27/1818C	1818-1830	Silver (89.3% Ag, 10.7% Cu)	5.383	24.0	1.1
O27/1846C	1846-1919	Silver (94.5% Ag, 5.5% Cu)	5.00	22.0	1.3
O27/1921C	1921-1930	Silver (72% Ag, 28% Cu)	5.00	22.0	1.4

11.1. O27/1817C 893‰ silver ½ Gulden (1817-1830)

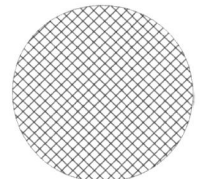

Issued with one obverse and one reverse design.

Obverse   *Reverse*

Obverse: Head of King Willem I facing right. Image from Verkade (1848).

Reverse: NL coat of arms between ½ and G. Image from Verkade (1848).

Type	Years	KM#	S#	Y#	X
O27/1817Cyyyy	1817-1830	54	30		

11.2. O27/1846C 945‰ silver ½ Gulden (1846-1919)

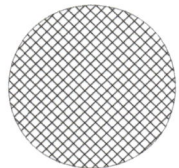

Issued with four obverse and three reverse designs. The second of this has two subtypes.

Obverse A

Obverse B

Obverse C

Obverse D

Obverse A: Head of King Willem II facing left.

Obverse B: Head of King Willem III facing right.

Obverse C: Head of Queen Wilhelmina designed for her inauguration facing left.

Obverse D: Head of Queen Wilhelmina wearing ermine coat facing left.

| *Reverse A* | *Reverse B²* | *Reverse C* |

Reverse A: NL coat of arms between "½" and "G".

Reverse B¹: NL coat of arms between "½" and "G" with narrow crown. "50 c." below coat of arms.

Reverse B²: As reverse B¹, but without "50 c." below coat of arms.

Reverse C: As reverse A with different crown, wider rim and different font type.

Type	Years	KM#	S#	Y#	X
O27/1846CyyyyAA	1846-1848	73	42		
O27/1846CyyyyBA	1850-1868	92	56	9	
O27/1846CyyyyCB¹	1898	121.1	72 (19th cent.), 7 (20th cent.)	25	
O27/1846CyyyyCB²	1904-1909	121.2	21	25a	
O27/1846CyyyyDC	1910-1919	147	36	41	

11.3. O27/1921C 720‰ silver ½ Gulden (1921-1930)

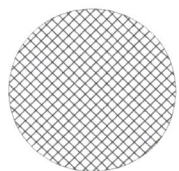

Issued with one obverse and one reverse design.

Obverse　　　　　*Reverse*

Obverse: Older head of Queen Wilhelmina facing left.

Reverse: NL coat of arms between "½" and "G".

Type	Years	KM#	S#	Y#	X
O27/1921Cyyyy	1921-1930	160	45	45	

12. O30/ 1 Gulden (NLG 1.00); 50 eurocent (EUR 0.50)

Although 50 eurocent is about 10% more than 1 Gulden they fall under the same heading as their nominal values are close enough to have the same logarithm after rounding. The Gulden was last minted in 2001 and removed from circulation in 2002, the 50 eurocent was first minted in 1999 and appeared in circulation in 2002. The 1 gulden denomination is the lowest that is not only issued as coins, but also as notes. These are all issued during periods of monetary difficulties, when either silver coins were hoarded or silver was not yet available for monetary purposes. A total of five coin series and six note series were issued with a face value of 1 Gulden. One series of 50 eurocent coins has been issued.

Series	Years	Comp.	Mass (g)	Size (mm)	THK (mm)
O30/1818C	1818-1837	Silver (89.3% Ag, 10.7% Cu)	10.766	30.0	1.6
O30/1840C	1840-1917	Silver (94.5% Ag, 5.5% Cu)	10.00	28.0	1.7
O30/1914N	1914	Paper		69x103	
O30/1916N	1618-1918	Paper		80x120	

Series	Years	Comp.	Mass (g)	Size (mm)	THK (mm)
O30/1920N	1920-1938	Paper		71x129	
O30/1922C	1922-1945	Silver (72% Ag, 28% Cu)	10.00	28.0	1.8
O30/1943N	1943	Paper		72x127	
O30/1945N	1945	Paper		60x114	
O30/1949N	1949	Paper		60x115	
O30/1954C	1954-1967	Silver (72% Ag, 28% Cu)	6.50	25.0	1.7
O30/1967C	1967-2001	Nickel (100% Ni)	6.00	25.0	1.7
O30/1999C	1999-....	Nordic gold (89% Cu, 5% Zn, 5% Al, 1% Sn)	7.80	24.25	2.38

12.1. O30/1818C 893‰ silver 1 Gulden (1818-1837)

Issued with one obverse and one reverse design.

Obverse   *Reverse*

Obverse: Head of King Willem I facing right. Image from Verkade (1848).

Reverse: NL coat of arms between "1" and "G". Image from Verkade (1848).

Type	Years	KM#	S#	Y#	X
O30/1818Cyyyy	1818-1837	55	31		

12.2. O30/1840C 945‰ silver 1 Gulden (1840-1917)

Issued with six obverse and three reverse designs. The second of this has two subtypes.

Obverse A   Obverse B   Obverse C

Obverse D   Obverse E   Obverse F

Obverse A: Head of King Willem I facing right. Image from Bonneville (1849).

Obverse B: Head of King Willem II facing left.

Obverse C: Head of King Willem III facing right.

Obverse D: Head of Queen Wilhelmina as a child with hair hanging down facing left.

Obverse E: Head of Queen Wilhelmina designed for her inauguration facing left.

Obverse F: Head of Queen Wilhelmina wearing ermine coat facing left.

Obverse A   *Reverse B²*   *Obverse C*

Reverse A: NL coat of arms between "1" and "G".

Reverse B¹: NL coat of arms between "1" and "G" with narrow crown. "100 c." below coat of arms.

Reverse B²: As reverse B¹, but without "100 c." below coat of arms.

Reverse C: As reverse A with different crown, wider rim and different font types.

Type	Years	KM#	S#	Y#	X
O30/1840CyyyyAA	1840	65	31		
O30/1840CyyyyBA	1840-1849	66	43		
O30/1840CyyyyCA	1850-1867	93	57	10	
O30/1840CyyyyDA	1892-1897	117	70	22	
O30/1840CyyyyEB¹	1898-1901	122.1	8 (20th cent.)	26	
O30/1840CyyyyEB²	1904-1909	121.2	21	25a	
O30/1840CyyyyFC	1910-1917	148	37	42	

12.3. O30/1914N 1ˢᵗ 1 Gulden silver certificate (1914)

Issued during the outbreak of World War I when silver coins disappeared from circulation due to hoarding.

The note is uniface (not printed on the back). Its dominant colour is brown.

This note is a silver certificate ("Zilverbon"), issued by the treasury of the Netherlands

Type	Date	P#	X
O30/1914N	7 August 1914	4	

12.4. O30/1916N 2ⁿᵈ 1 Gulden silver certificate (1916-1918)

Issued during World War I for the same reason as O30/1914N.

The note is also uniface but has a different design. Its dominant colour is brown.

This note is a silver certificate ("Zilverbon"), issued by the treasury of the Netherlands, with three different dates.

Type	Date	P#	X
O30/1916Nyyyy	1 May 1916, 1 November 1917, 1 October 1918	9, 11, 13	

12.5. O30/1920N 3ʳᵈ 1 Gulden silver certificate (1920, 1938)

This silver certificate is issued in two versions. Issued by the treasury of the Netherlands with three different dates.

The obverse is the same for both, but with different colours, the reverse is slightly different in the centre. The 1938 version is the 1 Gulden note that was in use during the occupation in World War II.

Obverse A²   *Reverse B*

Obverse A[1]: Brown on light green. Portrait of Queen Wilhelmina at left.

Obverse A[2]: As obverse A[1] but colour is brown only.

Reverse A: Text of penal code in centre of note.

Reverse B: Coat of arms of the Netherlands in centre with text of penal code below.

Type	Date	P#	X
O30/1920N1920A¹A	1 February 1920	15	
O30/1920N1938A²B	1 October 1938	61	

12.6. O30/1922C 720‰ silver 1 Gulden (1922-1945)

Issued with one obverse and one reverse design. The obverse design exists in two slightly different subtypes.

Obverse A¹   *Obverse A²*   *Reverse A*

Obverse A¹: Older head of Queen Wilhelmina facing left. Legend extends below head.

Obverse A²: As obverse A¹ but legend does not extend below head.

Reverse A: crowned NL coat of arms between "1" and "G".

Type	Years	KM#	S#	Y#	X
O30/1922CyyyyA¹A	1922-1944	161.1	46	46	
O30/1922CyyyyA²A	1944-1945	161.2	46	46	

12.7. O30/1943N WWII 1 Gulden treasury note (1943)

Printed in the USA during World War II to be used as emergency money once the Netherlands would be liberated. Issued by the Treasury. Issued and circulated mostly in the liberated southern part of the country.

Obverse   *Reverse*

Obverse: Red. Portrait of Queen Wilhelmina in centre of note.

Reverse: Orange. Coat of arms of the Netherlands in centre of note.

46

Type	Date	P#	X
O30/1943N	4 February 1943	64	

12.8. O30/1945N Post WWII Wilhelmina 1 Gulden treasury note (1945)

Printed in the UK and issued after the demonetisation of notes current during World War II. Issued by the Treasury.

Obverse   *Reverse*

Obverse: Brown on light green. Portrait of Queen Wilhelmina in centre of note.

Reverse: Brown. Coat of arms in centre of note.

Type	Date	P#	X
O30/1945N	18 May 1945	70	

12.9. O30/1949N Post WWII Juliana 1 Gulden treasury note (1949)

Printed in the Netherlands, issued after the inauguration of Queen Juliana as queen of the Netherlands.

Obverse   *Reverse*

Obverse: Brown on light green. Portrait of Queen Juliana at left.

Reverse: Brown. Large "1" in centre of note.

Type	Date	P#	X
O30/1949N	8 August 1949	72	

12.10. O30/1954C Small silver 1 Gulden (1954-1967)

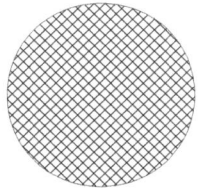

Issued with one obverse and one reverse type.

Obverse   *Reverse*

Obverse: Head of Queen Juliana facing right.

Reverse: NL coat of arms between "1" and "G".

Type	Years	KM#	S#	Y#	X
O30/1954Cyyyy	1954-1967	184	68	61	

12.11. O30/1967C Nickel 1 Gulden (1967-2001)

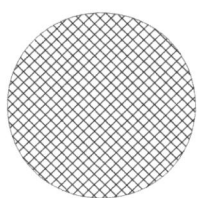

Issued with two obverse and two reverse permanent

designs. In this coin series two commemorative coins are issued. These are the lowest valued commemorative coins issued in the Netherlands.

Obverse A

Obverse B

Obverse A: Head of Queen Juliana facing right.

Obverse B: Head of Queen Beatrix facing left.

Reverse A

Reverse B

Reverse A: NL coat of arms between "1" and "G".

Reverse B: "1 G" on a grid representing the value.

Type	Years	KM#	S#	Y#	X
O30/1967CyyyyAA	1967-1980	184a	68a	61	
O30/1967CyyyyBB	1982-2001	205	85		
O30/1967CyyyyZZ	1980, 2001	Commemorative designs			

12.12. O30/1999C Nordic gold 50 eurocent (1999-....)

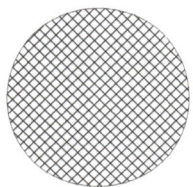

Two obverse types and two reverse types are issued until 2015.

Obverse A   *Obverse B*

Obverse A: Head of Queen Beatrix facing left.

Obverse B: Head of King Willem-Alexander facing right.

Reverse A   *Reverse B*

Reverse A: Value next to individually outlined European countries.

Reverse B: Value next to map of Europe.

Type	Years	KM#	S#	Y#	X
O30/1999CyyyyAA	1999-2006	239	122		
O30/1999CyyyyAB	2007-2013	270	154		
O30/1999CyyyyBB	2014-....				

13. O33/ 1 Euro (EUR 1.00)

Minted since 1999, in circulation since 2002 after the introduction of the Euro as the new European currency. Only one coin series has been produced since the introduction.

Series	Years	Comp.	Mass (g)	Size (mm)	THK (mm)
O33/1999C	1999-....	Bimetallic*	7.50 (core 3.79, ring 3.71)	23.25	2.33

*Ring: Nickel-brass (75% Cu, 20% Zn, 5% Ni). Core: Three layers. Outside layers copper-nickel (75% Cu, 25% Ni), central layer, 7% of thickness, pure nickel (100% Ni).

13.1. O33/1999C Bimetallic 1 Euro (1999-....)

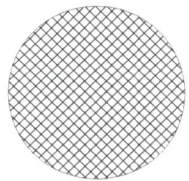

Two obverse types and two reverse types are issued until 2015.

Obverse A   *Obverse B*

Obverse A: Head of Queen Beatrix facing left.

Obverse B: Head of King Willem-Alexander facing right.

Reverse A   *Reverse B*

Reverse A: Value next to map of European Union.

Rev.erse B: Value next to map of Europe.

Type	Years	KM#	S#	Y#	X
O33/1999CyyyyAA	1999-2006	240	123		
O33/1999CyyyyAB	2007-2013	271	155		
O33/1999CyyyyBB	2014-....				

14. O34/ 2½ Gulden (NLG 2.50)

Minted for the first time in 1840 as replacement for the classic 3 Gulden coin that was issued already during the Dutch Republic. Last issued in 2001 and demonetised in 2002. The 2½ gulden denomination is issued as both coins and notes. All notes are issued during periods of monetary difficulties, when either silver coins were hoarded or silver was not yet available for monetary purposes. A total of four coin series and eight note series were issued with a face value of 2½ Gulden.

Series	Years	Comp.	Mass (g)	Size (mm)	THK (mm)
O34/1840C	1840-1898	Silver (94.5% Ag, 5.5% Cu)	25.0	38.0	2.5
O34/1846N	1846	Paper		85x167	
O34/1914N	1914	Paper		69x102	
O34/1915N	1915-1917	Paper		79x119	
O34/1918N	1918-1927	Paper		71x129	
O34/1929C	1929-1940	Silver (72% Ag, 28% Cu)	25.0	38.0	2.5

Series	Years	Comp.	Mass (g)	Size (mm)	THK (mm)
O34/1938N	1938	Paper		71x129	
O34/1943N	1943	Paper		71x127	
O34/1945N	1945	Paper		59x114	
O34/1949N	1949	Paper		60x115	
O34/1959C	1959-1966	Silver (72% Ag, 28% Cu)	15.0	33.0	2.2
O34/1969C	1969-2001	Nickel (100% Ni)	10.0	29.0	2.1

14.1. O34/1840C 945‰ silver 2½ Gulden (1840-1898)

Issued with four obverse and two reverse designs. The second obverse design has three different varieties.

Obverse A

Obverse B¹

Obverse B³

Obverse C

Obverse A: Head of King Willem I facing right. Image taken from counterfeit specimen.

Obverse B¹: Head of King Willem II facing left, signature "VAN DER KELLEN F.". Image from Bonneville (1849).

Obverse B²: As Obv. B¹ with ear higher, signature "VDK".

Obverse B³: As Obv. B¹ with 2 mm shorter neck. Sign. "VDK".

Obverse C: Head of King Willem III facing right.

Obverse D: Head of Queen Wilhelmina designed for her inauguration facing left.

Reverse A

Reverse A: NL coat of arms between "2½" and "G".

Reverse B: As Rev. A with narrow crown and different font type. Comparable to O30/1840-Rev. B.

Type	Years	KM#	S#	Y#	X
O34/1840CyyyyAA	1840	67	33		
O34/1840CyyyyB¹A	1841-1842	69	44		
O34/1840CyyyyB²A	1843-1845	69	44		
O34/1840CyyyyB³A	1846-1849	69	44		
O34/1840CyyyyCA	1849-1874	82	58	11	

Type	Years	KM#	S#	Y#	X
O34/1840CyyyyDB	1898	123	73 (19th cent.), 9 (20th cent.)	9	

14.2. O34/1846N 1846 2½ Gulden treasury note

Due to the introduction of the silver standard in 1850 large amounts of silver coins were necessary to exchange the gold coins that were no longer legal tender. As the production of large silver coins was not large enough paper money in the form of treasury notes were issued. The lowest in value for this was the 2½ Gulden treasury note. As it was only printed in 8000 copies it is however extremely rare (and missing from most catalogues).

Type	Date	P#	X
O34/1846N	1 January 1846		

14.3. O34/1914N 1st 2½ Gulden silver certificate (1914)

Issued during the outbreak of World War I when silver coins disappeared from circulation due to hoarding.

The note is uniface (not printed on the back). Its dominant colour is blue on green.

This note is a silver certificate ("Zilverbon"), issued by the treasury of the Netherlands.

Type	Date	P#	X
O34/1914N	7 August 1914	5	

14.4. O34/1915N 2nd 2½ Gulden silver certificate (1915-1917)

Issued during World War I for the same reason as O34/1914N.

The note is also printed on one side only but has a different design. Its dominant colour is blue.

This note is a silver certificate ("Zilverbon"), issued by the treasury of the Netherlands, with three different dates.

Type	Date	P#	X
O34/1915Nyyyy	30 March 1915, 31 March 1916, 1 August 1917	7, 8, 10	

14.5. O34/1918N 3rd 2½ Gulden silver certificate (1918-1927)

Issued after World War I until new silver 2½ Gulden coins with a lower silver content could be issued again. Issued with one obverse and two reverse designs.

Obverse A   Reverse A

Obverse A: "2.50" at left and in upper and lower right corners, large "2.50" in centre of note. Main colour blue on gray.

Reverse A: "2.50" in all corners. Diamond shape in centre with law article. Mostly blue, dark coloured.

Reverse B: Like Rev. A but main colour is light blue with white in centre.

Type	Date	P#	X
O34/1918NyyyyAA	1 July 1918, 1 October 1918, 1 October 1920	12, 14, 16	
O34/1918NyyyyAB	1 May 1922, 1 December 1922, 1 October 1923, 1 October 1927	17, 18, 19, 20	

14.6. O34/1929C 720‰ silver 2½ Gulden (1929-1940)

Issued with one obverse and one reverse designs. From the obverse two slightly different versions are minted.

Obverse A¹   *Obverse A²*   *Reverse A*

Obverse A¹: Older head of Queen Wilhelmina facing left.

Obverse A²: As obverse A¹ with coarser lining in hair.

Reverse A: NL coat of arms between "2½" and "G".

Type	Years	KM#	S#	Y#	X
O34/1929CyyyyA¹A	1929-1940	165	47	47	
O34/1929CyyyyA²A	1932-1938	165	47	47	

14.7. O34/1938N 3rd 2½ Gulden silver certificate (1938)

Although dated 1938 this 2½ Gulden silver certificate was only issued from 1940 and in use during the German occupation in World War II.

Issued with one obverse and reverse type and a fixed date.

Obverse *Reverse*

Obverse: Blue. "2.50" at left and in lower right corner. Large "2.50" in centre.

Reverse: Blue. Two circles with text in between with "2.50" in all four corners.

Type	Date	P#	X
O34/1938N	1 October 1938	62	

14.8. O34/1943N WWII 2½ Gulden treasury note (1943)

Printed in the USA during World War II to be used as emergency money once the Netherlands would be liberated. Issued by the Treasury. Issued and circulated mostly in the liberated southern part of the country.

Obverse *Reverse*

Obverse: Green. Portrait of Queen Wilhelmina in centre of

note.

Reverse: Orange. Coat of arms of the Netherlands in centre of note.

Type	Date	P#	X
O34/1943N	4 February 1943	65	

14.9. O34/1945N Post WWII Wilhelmina 2½ Gulden treasury note (1945)

Printed in the UK and issued after the demonetisation of notes current during World War II. Issued by the Treasury. Appears like 1 Gulden treasury note of 1945.

Obverse: Blue on violet. Portrait of Queen Wilhelmina in centre of note.

Reverse: Greyish blue. Coat of arms in centre of note.

Type	Date	P#	X
O34/1945N	18 May 1945	71	

14.10. O34/1949N Post WWII Juliana 2½ Gulden treasury note (1949)

Printed in the Netherlands, issued after the inauguration of Queen Juliana as queen of the Netherlands.

Obverse   *Reverse*

Obverse: Blue. Portrait of Queen Juliana at left.

Reverse: Blue. Large "2½" in centre of note.

Type	Date	P#	X
O34/1949N	8 August 1949	73	

14.11. O34/1959C Small silver 2½ Gulden (1959-1966)

Issued with one obverse and one reverse type.

Obverse   *Reverse*

Obverse: Head of Queen Juliana facing right.

Reverse: NL coat of arms between 2½ and G.

Type	Years	KM#	S#	Y#	X
O34/1959Cyyyy	1959-1966	185	69	62	

14.12. O34/1969C Nickel 2½ Gulden (1969-2001)

Issued with two obverse and two reverse permanent designs. In this coin series two commemorative coins were issued.

Obverse A   *Obverse B*

Obverse A: Head of Queen Juliana facing right.

Obverse B: Head of Queen Beatrix facing left.

Reverse A   *Reverse B*

Reverse A: NL coat of arms between "2½" and "G".

Reverse B: "2½ G" on a grid representing the value.

Type	Years	KM#	S#	Y#	X
O34/1969CyyyyAA	1969-1980	191	71		
O34/1969CyyyyBB	1982-2001	206	85		
O34/1969CyyyyZ	1979, 1980	Commemorative designs			

15. O35/ 3 Gulden (NLG 3.00)

The 3 Gulden coin was the continuation of the 3 gulden coin that circulated in the Dutch Republic. Only one coin series was issued

Series	Years	Comp.	Mass (g)	Size (mm)	THK (mm)
O35/1817C	1817-1832	Silver (89.3% Ag, 10.7% Cu)	32.298	40.0	2.3

61

15.1. O35/1817C Silver 3 Gulden (1817-1832)

This coin was replaced in 1840 by the 2½ Gulden coin. It was issued with one obverse and one reverse design.

Obverse   *Reverse*

Obverse: Head of King Willem I facing right. Image taken from counterfeit coin.

Reverse: NL coat of arms between "3" and "G". Image taken from counterfeit coin.

Type	Years	KM#	S#	Y#	X
O35/1817Cyyyy	1817-1832	49	34		

16. O36/ 2 Euro (EUR 2.00)

Minted since 1999, in circulation since 2002 after the introduction of the Euro as the new European currency. Only one coin series has been produced since the introduction.

Series	Years	Comp.	Mass (g)	Size (mm)	THK (mm)
O36/1999C	1999-....	Bimetallic*	8.50 (core 4.11, ring 4.39)	25.75	2.20

*Ring: Copper-nickel (75% Cu, 25% Ni). Core: Three layers. Outside layers nickel-brass (75% Cu, 20% Zn, 25% Ni), central layer, 12% of thickness, pure nickel (100% Ni).

16.1. O36/1999 Bimetallic 2 Euro (1999-....)

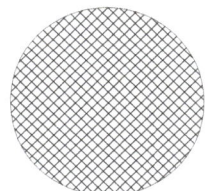

Two obverse types and two reverse types are issued until 2015. Since 2007 this series is used regularly for commemorative designs.

Obverse A   *Obverse B*

Obverse A: Head of Queen Beatrix facing left.

Obverse B: Head of King Willem-Alexander facing right.

Reverse A   *Reverse B*

Reverse A: Value next to map of European Union.

Reverse B: Value next to map of Europe.

Type	Years	KM#	S#	Y#	X
O36/1999CyyyyAA	1999-2006	240	123		
O36/1999CyyyyAB	2007-2013	271	155		
O36/1999CyyyyBB	2014-....				
O36/1999CyyyyZ	2007-....	Commemorative designs			

17. O37/ 5 Gulden (NLG 5.00)

The 5 Gulden denomination never was a popular one until the first appearance of bank notes of this denomination in 1966. Due to its high purchasing power there was for a long time no real need for a coin or note between the 2½ and 10 Gulden denominations. In spite of this it was issued in the form of coins or notes regularly between 1826 and 2001 when the Gulden was replaced by the Euro. A total of three coin and five note series were issued during this period.

Series	Years	Comp.	Mass (g)	Size (mm)	THK (mm)
O37/1826C	1826-1851	Gold (90% Au, 10% Cu)	3.3645	18.50	0.7
O37/1846N	1846	Paper		82x163	
O37/1912C	1912	Gold (90% Au, 10% Cu)	3.36	18.00	0.8
O37/1914N	1914	Paper		68x103	

Series	Years	Comp.	Mass (g)	Size (mm)	THK (mm)
O37/1944N	1944	Paper		71x127	
O37/1966N	1966	Paper		76x136	
O37/1973N	1973	Paper		76x136	
O37/1973C	1988-2001	Bronze plated nickel (100% Ni with 87.75% Cu and 12.25% Sn plating)	9.25	23.5	2.4

17.1. O37/1826C 1st gold 5 Gulden (1826-1851)

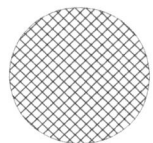

Issued with three obverse and two reverse designs. After 1850 no longer legal tender, but issued as bullion coin. For that reason no longer the nominal value but the gold content was written in the legend on the reverse. As these bullion coins were not popular only few are minted.

Obverse A   *Obverse B*   *Reverse A*

Obverse A: Head of King Willem I facing left. Image from Verkade (1848).

Obverse B: Head of King Willem II facing right. Image from Bonneville (1849).

Obverse C: Head of King Willem III facing left.

Reverse A: NL coat of arms between "5" and "G". Image from Verkade (1848).

Reverse B: NL coat of arms with weight and fineness in legend.

Type	Years	KM#	S#	Y#	X
O37/1826CyyyyAA	1826-1827	60	35		
O37/1826CyyyyBA	1843	72	45		
O37/1826CyyyyBB	1848	77	47A		
O37/1826CyyyyCB	1850-1851	94	60	12	

17.2. O37/1846N 1846 5 Gulden treasury note

Due to the introduction of the silver standard in 1850 large amounts of silver coins were necessary to exchange the gold coins that were no longer legal tender. As the production of large silver coins was not large enough paper money in the form of treasury notes were issued.

The note is printed on one side only and its colour is red.

Type	Date	P#	X
O37/1846N	1 January 1846	A11	

17.3. O37/1912C 2nd gold 5 Gulden (1912)

Issued for one year only.

Obverse   *Reverse*

Obverse: Head of Queen Wilhelmina facing right.

Reverse: NL coat of arms between "5" and "G".

Type	Years	KM#	S#	Y#	X
O37/1912Cyyyy	1912	151	41	31	

17.4. O37/1914N 1ˢᵗ 5 Gulden silver certificate

Issued during the outbreak of World War I when silver coins disappeared from circulation due to hoarding.

The note is uniface (only printed on the front). Its dominant colour is green. This note is a silver certificate ("Zilverbon"), issued by the treasury of the Netherlands.

Type	Date	P#	X
O37/1914N	7 August 1914	6	

17.5. O37/1944N 2ⁿᵈ 5 Gulden silver certificate

Issued during World War II through the occupying authorities. As the south of the country was liberated already this note only circulated in the northern part of the country.

| *Obverse* | *Reverse* |

Obverse: Green, large "5" to left and right of note.

Reverse: Gray, large "5" in centre.

Type	Date	P#	X
O37/1944N	16 October 1944	6	

17.6. O37/1966N 1ˢᵗ 5 Gulden banknote

Issued with a single date.

| *Obverse* | *Reverse* |

Obverse: Green, portrait of the poet Joost van den Vondel (1587-1679) at right.

Reverse: Green, stylised classic buildings at centre.

Type	Date	P#	X
O37/1966N	26 April 1966	90	

17.7. O37/1973N 2ⁿᵈ 5 Gulden banknote

Issued with a single date.

Obverse   *Reverse*

Obverse: Green, stylised portrait of the poet Joost van den Vondel (1587-1679) at right.

Reverse: Green, stylised pattern of lines.

Type	Date	P#	X
O37/1973N	28 March 1973	95	

17.8. O37/1988C Bronze plated nickel 5 Gulden (1988-2001)

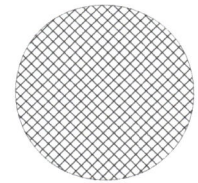

Due to inflation the 5 gulden bank notes only had a short lifetime during the 1980s and were replaced with a coin that would have a much longer lifetime. This coin series is issued with only one obverse and reverse regular design. It was issued once (in 2000) with a commemorative design.

Obverse   *Reverse*

Obverse: Head of Queen Beatrix facing left.

Reverse: "5 G" on a grid representing the value.

Type	Years	KM#	S#	Y#	X
O37/1988Cyyyy	1982-2001	210	87		
O37/1988CyyyyZ	2000	Commemorative design			

18. O40/ 10 Gulden (NLG 10.00); 5 Euro (EUR 5.00)

Although 5 Euro is about 10% more than 10 Gulden they fall under the same heading as their nominal values are close enough to have the same logarithm after rounding. 10 Gulden coins were issued in gold during the 19th and early 20th century. They were gradually replaced by bank notes during the first half of the 20th century. Silver 10 Gulden coins were issued during the second half of the 20th century for commemorative purposes only, although in relatively large mintages and issued at face value. The 5 Euro denomination is primarily issued as a note but also as commemorative coins. Although issued at face value they have much lower mintages and are rarely seen in circulation. A total of five coin series and 17 note series have been issued for 10 gulden and two coin series and two notes series have been issued for 5 Euro.

Series	Years	Comp.	Mass (g)	Size (mm)	THK (mm)
O40/1818C	1818-1851	Gold (90% Au, 10% Cu)	6.729	22.5	1.0
O40/1846N	1846	Paper		85x167	
O40/1849N	1849	Paper		130x196	
O40/1853N	1853-1875	Paper		100x160	
O40/1875C	1875-1933	Gold (90% Au, 10% Cu)	6.72	22.5	1.0
O40/1878N	1878-1892	Paper		125x179	
O40/1894N	1894-1903	Paper		95x170	

Series	Years	Comp.	Mass (g)	Size (mm)	THK (mm)
O40/1904N	1904-1923	Paper		96x170	
O40/1914N	1914	Paper		85x158	
O40/1924N	1924-1932	Paper		100x169	
O40/1933N	1933-1939	Paper		98x159	
O40/1940N	1940-1942	Paper		82x144	
O40/1943N[1]	1943-1944	Paper		68x143	
O40/1943N[2]	1943	Paper		72x151	
O40/1945N[1]	1945	Paper		71x133	
O40/1945N[2]	1945-1949	Paper		78x138	
O40/1953N	1953	Paper		83x147	
O40/1968N	1968	Paper		76x142	
O40/1970C	1970-1973	Silver (72% Ag, 28% Cu)	25.0	38.0	2.1
O40/1994C	1994	Silver (72% Ag, 28% Cu)	15.0	33.0	1.7
O40/1995C	1995-1999	Silver (80% Ag, 20% Cu)	15.0	33.0	1.7
O40/1997N	1997	Paper		76x136	
O40/2002N	2002	Paper		62x120	
O40/2003C	2003-2007	Silver (92.5% Ag, 7.5% Cu)	11.9	29.0	1.7
O40/2008C	2008-....	Silver plated copper	11.9	29.0	1.8
O40/2013N	2013	Paper		62x120	

18.1. O40/1818C 1st gold 10 gulden (1818-1851)

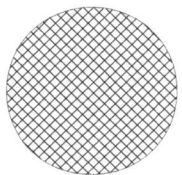

Issued with three obverse and two reverse designs. After 1850 no longer legal tender, but issued as bullion coin. For that reason no longer the nominal value but the gold content was written in the legend on the reverse. These bullion coins were not popular and as a result only few were minted.

Obverse A   *Obverse B*   *Reverse A*

Oveverse A: Head of King Willem I facing left. Image from Verkade (1848).

Obverse B: Head of King Willem II facing right. Image from Bonneville (1849).

Obverse C: Head of King Willem III facing left.

Reverse A: NL coat of arms between "10" and "G". Image from Verkade (1848).

Reverse B: NL coat of arms with weight and fineness in legend.

Type	Years	KM#	S#	Y#	X
O40/1818CyyyyAA	1818-1840	56	36		
O40/1818CyyyyBA	1842	71	46		

Type	Years	KM#	S#	Y#	X
O40/1818CyyyyBB	1848	78	47B		
O40/1818CyyyyCB	1850-1851	95	61	13	

18.2. O40/1846N 1846 10 Gulden treasury note

Due to the introduction of the silver standard in 1850 large amounts of silver coins were necessary to exchange the gold coins that were no longer legal tender. As the production of these large silver coins was not sufficient at first paper money in the form of treasury notes were issued.

The note is printed on one side only and its colour is brown.

Type	Date	P#	X
O40/1846N	1 January 1846	A12	

18.3. O40/1849N 1849 10 Gulden treasury note

Issued after the former note lost its value. Printed on one side only. The colour of this note is blue.

Type	Date	P#	X
O40/1849N	15 October 1849	A16	

18.4. O40/1853N 1853 10 gulden treasury note (1853-1875)

Issued after the former note lost its value. As the notes now were used to finance the state debt they could not be withdrawn and were issued for a considerable time with various signatures and dates. This note is also printed on one side only.

Type	Date	P#	X
O40/1853Nyyyy	Various dates between 1853 and 1875, 10 different signatures.	A20	

18.5. O40/1875C 2nd gold 10 gulden (1875-1933)

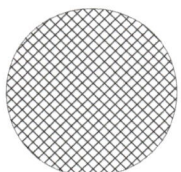

Issued when the Netherlands introduced the gold standard. Most of them were minted as backing for paper money and they did not see much circulation, resulting in the fact they they are still easy to obtain in good quality with small premiums over the gold spot prices. Issued with five different obverse and four different reverse designs. The first obverse design has two slightly different versions.

Obverse A¹   *Obverse A²*   *Obverse B*

Obverse D   *Obverse E*

Obverse A¹: Head of King Willem III facing right. Two

small stars in the legend.

Obverse A^2: Like obverse A^1 with larger stars in legend.

Obverse B: Head of Queen Wilhelmina as a child with hair hanging down facing left.

Obverse C: Head of Queen Wilhelmina designed for her inauguration facing right.

Obverse D: Head of Queen Wilhelmina wearing ermine coat facing right.

Obverse E: Older head of Queen Wilhelmina facing right.

Reverse A   *Reverse B*   *Reverse D*

Reverse A: NL coat of arms between "10" and "G". Mintage year at top, legend running below coat of arms.

Reverse B: As reverse A but mintage year at bottom and legend running above coat of arms.

Reverse C: As reverse B with smaller crown and different font in legend.

Reverse D: As reverse B with wider crown and another different font in legend.

Type	Years	KM#	S#	Y#	X
O40/1875CyyyyA^{1}A	1875	105	59	A16	
O40/1875CyyyyA^{2}B	1876-1889	106	59A	B16	
O40/1875CyyyyBB	1892-1897	118	71	28	
O40/1875CyyyyCC	1898	124	74 (19th cent.); 13 (20th cent.)	45	

Type	Years	KM#	S#	Y#	X
O40/1875CyyyyDD	1911-1917	149	42	30	
O40/1875CyyyyED	1925-1933	162	48	32	

18.6. O40/1878N 1878 10 Gulden treasury note (1878-1892)

New treasury note design. Now printed on both sides.

Obverse: Ornamental design with NL coat of arms at top.

Reverse : Large "10" in centre of note.

Type	Date	P#	X
O40/1878Nyyyy	Various dates between 1878 and 1892, 7 different signatures.	1	

18.7. O40/1894N Queen Wilhelmina 10 Gulden treasury note (1894-1903)

New design to incorporate the head of Queen Wilhelmina. Two obverse varieties, before and after the inauguration of the queen. The colour of these notes is brown.

Obverse A: "TIEN GULDEN" at centre with head of Queen as a child at right.

Obverse B: As obverse A with head of Queen Wilhelmina designed for her inauguration in 1898 at right.

Reverse A: Large "TIEN GULDEN" in centre with ornamental edges.

Type	Date	P#	X
O40/1894NyyyyAA	Various dates between 1894 and 1898, 4 different signature combinations.	2	
O40/1894NyyyyBA	Various dates between 1900 and 1903, 2 different signature combinations.	2A	

18.8. O40/1904 1904 10 gulden banknote (1904-1923)

In 1904 De Nederlandsche Bank took over the Dutch state debt. As a result the treasury notes (muntbiljetten) could be withdrawn and they were replaced by banknotes from De Nederlandsche Bank, which was now allowed to print banknotes with a nominal value of 10 Gulden. Before 1904 the lowest value a banknote could be was 25 Gulden. The first 10 Gulden banknote was issued with one obverse and one reverse design, both with two versions depending on the location of the serial numbers.

Obverse A^1: Two figures representing labour and prosperity with large "TIEN GULDEN" in the centre. Serial number on obverse.

Obverse A^2: As obverse A^1 but without serial number on obverse.

Reverse A: Large "TIEN GULDEN" in centre and "10"s in upper left and lower right corner.

Reverse B: Like reverse A but with "10"s in all corners.

Type	Date	P#	X
O40/1904NyyyyA^{1}A	Various dates between 1904 and 1921, 4 different signature combinations.	34	
O40/1904NyyyyA^{2}B	Various dates between 1921 and 1923, one signature combination.	35	

18.9. O40/1914 1914 10 Gulden emergency banknote

Designed, printed and issued in a hurry due to fast disappearance of gold coins from circulation after the start of World War I. Apparently due to stabilisation of the situation only a small number needed to be issued.

Obverse: Red coloured, large "TIEN GULDEN" in centre.

Reverse: Very vague light blue, "TIEN GULDEN" in centre.

Type	Date	P#	X
O40/1914N	1 August 1914	28	

18.10. O40/1924N 1924 10 Gulden banknote (1924-1932)

Within this series small variety changes in the reverse appear due to changes in the text of the penal code.

Obverse A: Zeeland farmer's wife with "TIEN GULDEN" above.

Reverse A[1]: Ornamental design. Penal code text left and right starts with "Het in voorraad ...".

Reverse A[2]: Ornamental design. Penal code text left and right starts with "Het namaken of ...".

Reverse A[3]: Ornamental design. Penal code text left and right starts with "WETBOEK VAN STRAFRECHT ...".

Type	Date	P#	X
O40/1924NyyyyAA[1]	Various dates between 1924 and 1926, one signature combination.	46a	
O40/1924NyyyyAA[2]	Various dates between 1926 and 1932, two signature combinations.	46b, 46c	
O40/1924NyyyyAA[3]	Various dates in 1932, one signature combination.	46d	

18.11. O40/1933N 1933 10 Gulden banknote (1933-1939)

One design. The date is variable.

| *Obverse* | *Reverse* |

Obverse: Head of old man at right.

Reverse: Ornamental design.

Type	Date	P#	X
O40/1933Nyyyy	Various dates between 1933 and 1939, one signature combination.	52	

18.12. O40/1940N 1st WWII 10 gulden banknote (1940-1942)

Issued with two different obverse designs. The original with Queen Emma (the mother of Queen Wilhelmina) was not allowed to circulate by the German occupiers, and a different design was developed. Due to later banknote shortages it was allowed to circulate with the excuse that Emma was of German descent.

| *Obverse B* | *Reverse A* |

Obverse A: Head of Queen Emma (1858-1934) at right. Mostly brown/green.

Obverse B: Head of girl with grapes at right. Mostly blue/green.

Reverse A: Ornamental design.

Type	Date	P#	X
O40/1940NyyyyAA	Various dates between 1940 and 1941, one signature combination.	56	
O40/1940NyyyyBA	Various dates between 1940 and 1942, two signature combinations.	55	

18.13. O40/1943N¹ 2ⁿᵈ WWII 10 Gulden banknote (1943-1944)

Due to paper shortages a new banknote was designed with a lower height so that more notes could be cut from a sheet.

Obverse   *Reverse*

Obverse: Portrait of Volckert Jansz (1610-1681), taken from Rembrandt's painting "Syndics of the Drapers' Guild".

Reverse: Ornamental design.

Type	Date	P#	X
O40/1943N¹	Various dates between 1943 and 1944, one signature combination.	60	

18.14. O40/1943N² WWII 10 Gulden treasury note (1943)

Printed in the USA during World War II to be used as emergency money once the Netherlands would be liberated. Issued by the Treasury. Issued and circulated mostly in the liberated southern part of the country.

Obverse: Blue. Portrait of Queen Wilhelmina in centre of

note.

Reverse: Orange. Coat of arms of the Netherlands in centre of note.

Type	Date	P#	X
O40/1943N²	4 February 1943	66	

18.15. O40/1945N¹ "Lieftincktientje" (1945)

Designed and printed in the Netherlands after WWII because the regular banknote supply from the UK did not arrive in time for the scheduled monetary reform.

Obverse: Stylised lion below "TIEN GULDEN". Mostly blue.

Reverse: Ornamental design. Red and blue.

Type	Date	P#	X
O40/1945N¹	7 May 1945	74	

18.16. O40/1945N² 1945 10 Gulden banknote (1945-1949)

Issued with one obverse and two different reverse designs. Due to an error in the first obverse design and a colour change in 1949 there are three subtypes of this design. Printed in England.

Obverse A¹: Dark blue, head of King Willem I at right. Wrong birth year of King: 1788

Obverse A²: Dark blue, head of King Willem I at right, corrected birth year: 1772.

Obverse A³: Blue, head of King Willem I at right.

Reverse A: Colliery.

Reverse B: Landscape with windmill.

Type	Date	P#	X
O40/1945N²yyyyA¹A	7 May 1945	75a	
O40/1945N²yyyyA²A	7 May 1945	75b	
O40/1945N²yyyyA³B	4 March 1949	83	

18.17. O40/1953N 1953 10 Gulden banknote

One design, fixed date and signatures.

Obverse   *Reverse*

Obverse: Head of the jurist Hugo de Groot (1583-1645) at right.

Reverse: Scale at left.

Type	Date	P#	X
O40/1953N	23 March 1953	86	

18.18. O40/1968N 1968 10 Gulden banknote

One design, fixed date and signatures.

 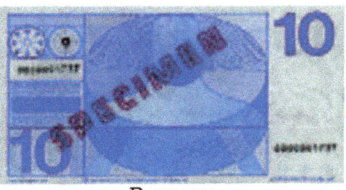

Obverse   *Reverse*

Obverse: Blue, stylised portrait of the painter Frans Hals (1582-1666) at right. Image from ECB website.

Reverse: Blue, stylised pattern of lines. Image from ECB website.

Type	Date	P#	X
O40/1968N	25 April 1968	91	

18.19. O40/1970C Large silver 10 Gulden (1970-1973)

Issued as (2) commemorative coins only.

18.20. O40/1994C 720‰ small silver 10 Gulden (1994)

Commemorative issue for one year only.

18.21. O40/1995C 800‰ small silver 10 Gulden (1995-1999)

Increased silver fineness to be within the internationally acceptable range for silver coins. Issued as (4) commemorative coins only.

18.22. O40/1997N 1997 10 gulden banknote

One design, fixed date and signature.

Obverse   *Reverse*

Obverse: Blue, design representative for a kingfisher bird. Image from ECB website.

Reverse: Blue, abstract design. Image from ECB website.

Type	Date	P#	X
O40/1997N	1 July 1997		

18.23. O40/2002N 1ˢᵗ series 5 Euro banknote (2002)

One design, two signature variations. Printed mostly in grey.

Obverse   *Reverse*

Obverse: Classical architecture. Image from ECB website.

Reverse: Map of Europe with classical aqueduct. Image from ECB website.

Type	Signatures	P#	X
O40/2002Nyyyy	Duisenberg (2002), Trichet (2004)	1, 8	

18.24. O40/2003C Silver 5 Euro (2003-2007)

Issued as (8) commemorative coins only.

18.25. O40/2008C Silver plated copper 5 Euro (2008-....)

Due to rapidly increasing silver prices in 2007 it was no longer possible to issue the silver coins at face value. For that reason it was decided to change the composition of the regular commemorative version to silver plated copper. As a result of this change the silver content of these coins is less than 5 %. Issued as commemorative coins only at a rate of 2 or 3 per year.

18.26. O40/2013N Europa series 5 Euro banknote (2013)

One design, all with the signature of M. Draghi. Printed mostly in grey.

Obverse   *Reverse*

Obverse: Classical architecture, location of design elements changed, larger "5". Image from ECB website.

Reverse: Map of Europe with classical aqueduct. Location of design elements changed from previous series. Image from ECB website.

Type	Signature	P#	X
O40/2013Nyyyy	M. Draghi (2013)	21	

19. O43/ 20 Gulden (NLG 20.00); 10 Euro (EUR 10.00)

As with other denominations 20 Gulden and the nominally slightly larger 10 Euro fall under the same header. 20 Gulden never was a popular denomination in the Netherlands. Except for rare notes and coins from the 19th century it was issued as banknotes between 1926 and 1955, but as its value was too close to the more popular 25 Gulden it did not serve any real need. In the Euro series the 10 Euro denomination is a very logical denomination and it is used for both bank notes and the occasional commemorative coins. One 20 Gulden coin series and five note series, and two 10 Euro note and coin series exist.

Series	Years	Comp.	Mass (g)	Size (mm)	THK (mm)
O43/1846N	1846	Paper		85x167	
O43/1848C	1848-1853	Gold (90% Au, 10% Cu)	13.458	27	1.4
O43/1926N	1926-1938	Paper		89x170	
O43/1939N	1939-1941	Paper		82x155	
O43/1945N	1945	Paper		85x150	
O43/1955N	1955	Paper		82x151	
O43/2002C	2002-2005	Silver (92.5% Ag, 7.5% Cu)	17.8	33.0	2.0
O43/2002N	2002	Paper		67x127	
O43/2013C	2013-....	Silver plated copper	15.5	33.0	2.0
O43/2014N	2014	Paper		67x127	

19.1. O43/1846N 1846 20 Gulden treasury note

Due to the introduction of the silver standard in 1850 large amounts of silver coins were necessary to exchange the gold coins that were no longer legal tender. As the production of large silver coins was not large enough paper money in the form of treasury notes were issued.

The note is printed on one side only and its colour is green.

Type	Date	P#	X
O43/1846N	1 January 1846	A13	

19.2. O43/1848 Gold 20 gulden (1848-1853)

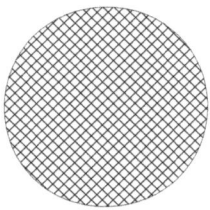

When it was decided to abolish the legal tender status of the gold coins in the 1840s it was also decided that the coins could continue to circulate as trade coins. This would be reflected in newly minted coins by replacing the nominal value with the gold fineness and weight. It was also decided to extend the array of gold coins with a coin double the weight of the 10 Gulden coin. These trade coins proved not popular and as a result only very few were minted. As a result this series is one of the rarest Netherlands coin series. Minted with two obverse and one reverse design.

Reverse A: Head of King Willem II facing right.

Reverse B: Head of King Willem III facing left.

Obverse A: NL coat of arms with weight and fineness in legend.

Type	Years	KM#	S#	Y#	X
O43/1848CyyyyAA	1848	79	47C		
O43/1848CyyyyBA	1850-1853	96	62	14	

19.3. O43/1926N 1926 20 gulden banknote (1926-1938)

First 20 Gulden banknote after the lower limit for banknotes was decreased from 25 to 10 Gulden in 1904. One obverse and reverse design.

Obverse   *Reverse*

Obverse: Sailor, "20" in all four corners. Mostly green.

Reverse: Ornamental design with repeating "20".

Type	Date	P#	X
O43/1926Nyyyy	Various dates between 1926 and 1938, two signature combinations	47	

19.4. O43/1939N 1939 20 Gulden banknote (1939-1941)

One obverse and reverse design.

Obverse   *Reverse*

Obverse: Queen Emma (1858-1934) at right, ships left. Mostly violet.

Reverse: Building at left and right. Centre ornamental.

Type	Date	P#	X
O43/1939Nyyyy	Various dates between 1939 and 1941, one signature combination	53, 54	

19.5. O43/1945N 1945 20 Gulden banknote

One obverse and reverse design, fixed date.

Obverse: Prince Willem III, the later king of England

(1650-1702) at right, brown and green.

Reverse: Moerdijk bridge (the first bridge between the nother and southern part of the Netherlands), printed in green and yellow.

Type	Date	P#	X
O43/1945N	7 May 1945	76	

19.6. O43/1953N 1953 20 Gulden banknote

One obverse and reverse design. It was taken out of circulation in 1961 as it served no need compared to the more popular 25 gulden banknote.

Obverse: Portrait of the physisian and botanist Herman Boerhaave (1668-1738) at right. Mostly lilac, green and brown.

Reverse: Snake with wine glass, on ornamental design. Lilac and grey.

Type	Date	P#	X
O43/1953N	8 November 1955	88	

19.7. O43/2002C Silver 10 Euro (2002-2005)

Issued as (3) commemorative coins only.

19.8. O43/2002N 1ˢᵗ series 10 Euro banknote (2002)

One design, three signature variations. Printed mostly in red.

Obverse   *Reverse*

Obverse: Romanesque architecture. Image from ECB website.

Reverse: Map of Europe with Romanesque bridge. Image from ECB website.

Type	Signatures	P#	X
O43/2002Nyyyy	Duisenberg (2002), Trichet (2004), Draghi (2012)	2, 9, 15	

19.9. O43/2013C Silver plated copper 10 Euro (2013-....)

Until 2015 issued as (1) commemorative coin only.

19.10. O43/2014N Europa series 10 Euro banknote (2014)

One design, all with the signature of M. Draghi. Printed

mostly in red.

Obverse   *Reverse*

Obverse: Romanesque architecture, location of design elements changed, larger "10". Image from ECB website.

Reverse: Map of Europe with Romanesque bridge. Location of design elements changed from previous series. Image from ECB website.

Type	Signatures	P#	X
O43/2014Nyyyy	Draghi (2014)	22	

20. O44/ 25 Gulden (NLG 25.00)

Issued as 13 note series. These are mostly banknotes as the 25 Gulden denomination was the lowest value a banknote could be before 1904. No coin series.

Series	Years	Comp.	Mass (g)	Size (mm)	THK (mm)
O44/1814N	1814-1862	Paper		Various	
O44/1861N	1861-1921	Paper		105x220	
O44/1914N	1914	Paper		90x162	
O44/1921N	1921-1930	Paper		101x174	
O44/1931N	1931-1941	Paper		77x163	
O44/1940N	1940-1944	Paper		89x158	
O44/1943N	1943	Paper		72x152	
O44/1945N	1945	Paper		82x133	
O44/1947N	1947	Paper		87x155	
O44/1949N	1949	Paper		81x146	
O44/1955N	1955	Paper		87x155	

Series	Years	Comp.	Mass (g)	Size (mm)	THK (mm)
O44/1971N	1971	Paper		76x148	
O44/1989N	1989	Paper		71x140	

20.1. O44/1814N 1814 25 Gulden banknote (1814-1862)

Issued between 1814 and 1862. Although 7 to 8 slightly different versions were issued they all have hand written signatures. These notes looked like cheques and are printed in a large variety of font types and have an ornamental edge consisting of musical notes. They are printed on one side only.

Type	Signatures	P#	X
O44/1814Nyyyy	Several date and signature varieties.	A1, A2	

20.2. O44/1861N 1861 25 Gulden banknote (1861-1921)

Printed on one side only. Signatures are printed.

Obverse: Coat of Arms at top, "25" in all four corners. The colour is red.

Type	Dates / Signatures	P#	X
O44/1861Nyyyy	Various dates between 1861 and 1921, ten signature combinations.	21	

20.3. O44/1914N 1914 25 Gulden emergency banknote

Designed, printed and issued in a hurry due to fast disappearance of gold coins from circulation after the start of World War I. Apparently due to stabilisation of the situation only a small number needed to be issued.

Obverse: Green coloured, large "VIJF EN TWINTIG

GULDEN" in centre.

Reverse: Very vague light green, "VIJF EN TWINTIG GULDEN" in centre.

Type	Date	P#	X
O44/1914N	1 August 1914	29	

20.4. O44/1921N 1921 25 Gulden banknote (1921-1930)

Issued with one obverse in two varieties with different colours and two different reverse designs. Due to a change in the text of the penal code two versions of the first reverse exist with different texts.

Obverse A: Red coloured note with Prince Willem I on top and numeral "25" in each corner.

Obverse B: Same design as obverse A but printed in blue.

Reverse A^1: Building of "De Nederlandsche Bank". Two "25"s at upper left and right. The text of the penal code starts with "Het in voorraad hebben ..."

Reverse A^2: Like reverse A^1 but text of penal code starts with "Het namaken ..."

Reverse B: Picture of building removed, "25"s larger and at centre left and right.

Type	Dates / Signatures	P#	X
O44/1921NyyyyAA^1	Various dates between 1921 and 1923, one signature combination.	36	
O44/1921NyyyyAA^2	Various dates in February 1926, one signature combination.	36	
O44/1921NyyyyBB	Various dates in 1927 and 1928, one signature combination.	38	
O44/1921NyyyyAB	Various dates in 1929 and 1930, one signature variation.	37	

20.5. O44/1931N 1931 25 Gulden banknote (1931-1941)

One obverse and one reverse only. Printed in red.

Obverse   *Reverse*

Obverse: Head of the President of "De Nederlandsche Bank" W.C. Mees (1813-1884), President of "De Nederlandsche Bank" at left.

Reverse: Ornamental design with numeral "25" in all four corners.

Type	Dates / Signatures	P#	X
O44/1931Nyyyy	Various dates between 1931 and 1941, two signature combinations.	21	

20.6. O44/1940N 1940 25 Gulden banknote (1940-1944)

Issued with two different obverse designs. The original obverse had an orange colour and this could be related to the royal house of the Netherlands. For that reason it was replaced by a more reddish design later during World War II.

Obverse A: Head of Princess of Nassau-Dietz at right. Yellowish orange colour.

Obverse B: Like obverse A but colour more red-brown. Picture wider and with DNB monogram at left.

Reverse A: Ornamental design, printed in brown, blue and green.

Type	Dates / Signatures	P#	X
O44/1940NyyyyAA	20 May 1940. One signature combination.	57	
O44/1940NyyyyBA	Various dates in 1943 and 1944. One signature combination.	58	

20.7. O44/1943N WWII 25 Gulden treasury note (1943)

Printed in the USA during World War II to be used as emergency money once the Netherlands would be liberated. Issued by the Treasury. Issued and circulated mostly in the liberated southern part of the country. It is the only note of this denomination that is not a banknote but a treasury note.

Obverse: Olive. Portrait of Queen Wilhelmina in centre of note.

Reverse: Orange. Coat of arms of the Netherlands in centre of note.

Type	Date	P#	X
O44/1943N	4 February 1943	67	

20.8. O44/1945N 1945 25 gulden banknote

Issued with one design and a fixed date.

Obverse: Lilac and yellow. Girl's head at right.

Reverse: Ornamental design showing the head of a fish at the top and a shell at the bottom. Printed in red-brown, lilac and green.

Type	Date	P#	X
O44/1945N	7 May 1945	77	

20.9. O44/1947N 1947 25 Gulden banknote

Issued with one design and a fixed date.

Obverse: Head of King Salomon at right. Printed in orange.

Reverse: Ornamental design, printed in orange, blue and brown.

Type	Date	P#	X
O44/1947N	1 July 1949	84	

20.10. O44/1955N 1955 25 Gulden banknote

Issued with one design and a fixed date.

Obverse   *Reverse*

Obverse: Head of the scientist Christiaan Huygens (1629-1695) at right. Printed in red, orange and green.

Reverse: Ornamental design, printed in lilac, red and green.

Type	Date	P#	X
O44/1955N	10 April 1955	87	

20.11. O44/1971N 1971 25 Gulden banknote

Issued in one design only with a fixed date.

Obverse   *Reverse*

Obverse: Stylised head of composer Jan Pietersz Sweelinck 1562-1621) at right. Printed mostly in red.

Reverse: Ornamental design. Mostly printed in red.

Type	Date	P#	X
O44/1971N	10 February 1971	92	

20.12. O44/1989N 1989 25 Gulden banknote

Issued in one design only with a fixed date.

Obverse   *Reverse*

Obverse: Red, design indicative for a robin. Image from ECB website.

Reverse: Red, abstract design. Image from ECB website.

Type	Date	P#	X
O44/1971N	5 April 1989	100	

21. O46/ 40 Gulden (NLG 40.00); 20 Euro (EUR 20.00)

40 Gulden was a regular banknote denomination issued by De Nederlandsche Bank between 1814 and 1927, when it was abolished. 20 Euro is a regular denomination since the introduction of the Euro in 2002. Both are only issued

as banknotes in a total of six designs.

Series	Years	Comp.	Mass (g)	Size (mm)	THK (mm)
O46/1814N	1814-1862	Paper		Various	
O46/1860N	1860-1923	Paper		105x220	
O46/1914N	1914	Paper		96x166	
O46/1923N	1923-1927	Paper		100x175	
O46/2002N	2002	Paper		72x133	
O46/2015N	2015	Paper		72x133	

21.1. O46/1814N 1814 40 Gulden banknote (1814-1862)

Issued between 1814 and 1862. Although 6 slightly different versions were issued they all have hand written signatures. These notes looked like cheques and are printed in a large variety of font types and have an ornamental edge consisting of musical notes. They are printed in orange on one side only.

Type	Signatures	P#	X
O46/1814Nyyyy	Several date and signature varieties.	A1, A3	

21.2. O46/1861N 1861 40 Gulden banknote (1861-1921)

Printed on one side only. Signatures are printed.

Obverse: Coat of Arms at top, "40" in all four corners. The colour is green.

Type	Dates / Signatures	P#	X
O46/1861Nyyyy	Various dates between 1861 and 1921, seven signature combinations.	22	

21.3. O46/1914N 1914 40 Gulden emergency banknote

Designed, printed and issued in a hurry due to fast disappearance of gold coins from circulation after the start of World War I. Apparently due to stabilisation of the situation only a small number needed to be issued.

Obverse: Light green coloured, large "VEERTIG GULDEN" in centre.

Reverse: Very vague light blue, "VEERTIG GULDEN" in centre.

Type	Date	P#	X
O46/1914N	1 August 1914	30	

21.4. O46/1923N 1923 40 Gulden banknote (1923-1927)

Issued in one design with different dates. Printed in green. Due to a change in the text of the anti counterfeiting law two slightly different reverse versions have been issued.

Obverse A: Head of Prince Maurits at top. Numeral "40"s in all four corners.

Reverse A[1]: Building of "De Nederlandsche Bank" in centre of note. Two "40"s at upper left and right. Penal code text starts with "Hij die bankbiljetten ...".

Reverse A[2]: As Rev. A[1] but text of penal code starts with "Het namaken of ...".

Type	Dates / Signatures	P#	X
O46/1923NyyyyAA[1]	Various dates between 1923 and 1925, one signature combination.	39	
O46/1923NyyyyAA[2]	Various dates in 1927, one signature combination.	39	

21.5. O46/2002N 1ˢᵗ series 20 Euro banknote (2002)

One design, three signature variations. Printed mostly in blue.

Obverse   *Reverse*

Obverse: Gothic style architecture. Image from ECB website.

Reverse: Map of Europe with Gothic style bridge. Image from ECB website.

Type	Signatures	P#	X
O46/2002Nyyyy	Duisenberg (2002), Trichet(2004), Draghi (2012)	3, 10, 16	

21.6. O46/2015N Europa series 20 Euro banknote (2015)

One design, all with the signature of M. Draghi. Printed mostly in blue.

Obverse   *Reverse*

Obverse: Gothic style architecture, location of design elements changed, larger "20". Image from ECB website.

Reverse: Map of Europe with Gothic style bridge. Location of design elements changed from previous series. Image from ECB website.

Type	Signatures	P#	X
O46/2015Nyyyy	Draghi (2015)	23	

22. O47/ 50 Gulden (NLG 50.00)

The 50 Gulden denomination was only used as a treasury note during the 19th century. During this period there was no need for a 50 Gulden banknote as 40, 60 and 80 Gulden banknotes were issued. Only in 1929, after the discontinuation of the 40, 60 and 80 Gulden banknotes the first 50 Gulden banknote was issued. Again this was discontinued shortly after World War II. Due to inflation and to avoid extensive wear for the popular 25 Gulden banknote in 1982 again 50 Gulden banknotes were issued. As a result eight different 50 Gulden series have been issued, three treasury note and four banknote series. Since 1982 the 50 Gulden denomination was also used to issue face value commemorative coins. As such this it the largest coin denomination ever issued at face value.

Series	Years	Comp.	Mass (g)	Size (mm)	THK (mm)
O47/1854N	1854	Paper		98x159	
O47/1885N	1885-1897	Paper		95x170	
O47/1929N	1929-1931	Paper		101x142	
O47/1941N	1941	Paper		94x165	
O47/1943N	1943	Paper		72x152	
O47/1945N	1945	Paper		70x150	
O47/1982C	1982-1998	Silver (92.5% Ag, 7.5% Cu)	25.0	38.0	2.1
O47/1982N	1982	Paper		76x147	

22.1. O47/1854N 1854 50 gulden treasury note

This note is printed on one side only. Design equal to 1853 10 Gulden treasury note.

Type	Date	P#	X
O47/1854Nyyyy	Various dates in 1854, two different signatures.		

22.2. O47/1885N 1885 50 Gulden treasury note (1885-1897)

Now printed on both sides. New design to incorporate the head of King Willem III at right. The colour of these notes is green.

Obverse: "VIJFTIG GULDEN" at centre with head of KING WILLEM III at right.

Reverse: Large "50 GULDEN" in centre with ornamental edges.

Type	Date	P#	X
O47/1885Nyyyy	Various dates between 1885 and 1897, four different signature combinations.	3	

22.3. O47/1929N 1929 50 Gulden banknote (1929-1931)

Printed in one design with several issue dates.

Obverse: Head of Minerva at right. Printed in gray-blue.

Reverse: Ornamental design. Printed in green-orange.

Type	Date	P#	X
O47/1929Nyyyy	Various dates between 1929 and 1931, one signature combination.	47	

22.4. O47/1941N 1941 50 gulden banknote

Printed in one design with several issue dates.

Obverse: Printed in red and brown. Head of woman to left and right.

Reverse: Winter landscape, "50"s in each corner.

Type	Date	P#	X
O47/1941Nyyyy	Various dates in 1941, one signature combination.	59	

22.5. O47/1943N WWII 50 Gulden treasury note (1943)

Printed in the USA during World War II to be used as emergency money once the Netherlands would be liberated. Issued by the Treasury. Issued and circulated mostly in the liberated southern part of the country.

Obverse: Brown. Portrait of Queen Wilhelmina in centre of note.

Reverse: Orange. Coat of arms of the Netherlands in centre of note.

Type	Date	P#	X
O47/1943N	4 February 1943	68	

22.6. O47/1945N 1945 50 Gulden banknote

Issued with one design and a fixed date.

Obverse: Head of Prince Willem II (1626-1650) as a youth at right.

Reverse: Ornamental design with "50" in centre.

Type	Date	P#	X
O47/1945N	7 May 1945	78	

22.7. O47/1982C Silver 50 Gulden (1982-1998)

Issued as (7) commemorative coins only.

22.8. O47/1982N 1982 50 gulden banknote

Issued with one design and a fixed date.

Obverse   *Reverse*

Obverse: Sun flower. Main colour yellow. Image from ECB website.

Reverse: Map of the province of Flevoland with field of sun flowers. Mostly yellow and green. Image from ECB website.

Type	Date	P#	X
O47/1945N	4 January 1982	96	

23. O48/ 60 Gulden (NLG 60.00)

Issued as banknotes in four series between 1914 and 1927.

Series	Years	Comp.	Mass (g)	Size (mm)	THK (mm)
O48/1814N	1814-1862	Paper		Various	
O48/1860N	1860-1923	Paper		105x220	
O48/1914N	1914	Paper		100x172	
O48/1923N	1923-1927	Paper		100x175	

23.1. O48/1814N 1814 60 Gulden banknote (1814-1862)

Issued between 1814 and 1862. Although six slightly different versions were issued they all have hand written signatures. These notes looked like cheques and are printed in a large variety of font types and have an ornamental edge consisting of musical notes. They are printed in lilac on one side only.

Type	Signatures	P#	X
O48/1814Nyyyy	Several date and signature varieties.	A1, A4	

23.2. O48/1861N 1861 60 Gulden banknote (1861-1921)

Printed on one side only. Signatures are printed.

Obverse: Coat of Arms at top, "60" in all four corners. The colour is lilac.

Type	Dates / Signatures	P#	X
O48/1861Nyyyy	Various dates between 1861 and 1923, six signature combinations.	23	

23.3. O48/1914N 1914 60 Gulden emergency banknote

Designed, printed and issued in a hurry due to fast disappearance of gold coins from circulation after the start of World War I. Apparently due to stabilisation of the situation only a small number needed to be issued.

Obverse: Brown on green, large "ZESTIG GULDEN" in centre.

Reverse: Very vague light blue, "ZESTIG GULDEN" in centre.

Type	Date	P#	X
O48/1914N	1 August 1914	31	

23.4. O48/1923N 1923 60 Gulden banknote (1923-1927)

Issued in one design with different dates. Printed in lilac. Due to a change in the text of the anti counterfeiting law two slightly different reverse versions have been issued.

Obverse A: Head of Prince Frederik Hendrik (1584-1647) at top. Numeral "60"s in all four corners.

Reverse A[1]: Building of "De Nederlandsche Bank" in centre of note. Two "60"s at upper left and right. Penal code text starts with "Hij die bankbiljetten ...".

Reverse A[2]: As reverse A[1] but text of penal code starts with "Het namaken of ...".

Type	Dates / Signatures	P#	X
O48/1923NyyyyAA[1]	Various dates in 1923 and 1924, one signature combination.	40	
O48/1923NyyyyAA[2]	Various dates in 1927, one signature combination.	40	

24. O49/ 80 Gulden (NLG 80.00)

Only issued in the first banknote series of De Nederlandsche Bank.

Series	Years	Comp.	Mass (g)	Size (mm)	THK (mm)
O49/1814N	1814-1830	Paper		Various	

24.1. O49/1814N 1814 80 Gulden banknote (1814-1830)

Issued between 1814 and approximately 1830. Although four slightly different versions were issued they all have hand written signatures. These notes looked like cheques and are printed in a large variety of font types and have an ornamental edge consisting of musical notes. They are printed in lilac on one side only.

Type	Signatures	P#	X
O49/1814Nyyyy	Several date and signature varieties.	A1, A5	

25. O50/ 100 Gulden (NLG 100.00); 50 Euro (EUR 50)

100 Gulden is issued as four treasury note and eleven banknote series. 50 Euro is issued as one banknote series.

Series	Years	Comp.	Mass (g)	Size (mm)	THK (mm)
O50/1814N	1814-1860	Paper		Various	
O50/1846N	1846	Paper		85x167	
O50/1849N	1849	Paper		130x196	
O50/1853N	1853	Paper		120x220	
O50/1860N	1860-1921	Paper		120x220	
O50/1914N	1914	Paper		130x210	
O50/1922N	1922-1929	Paper		122x215	
O50/1930N	1930-1944	Paper		100x175	
O50/1943N	1943	Paper		72x152	
O50/1945N	1945	Paper		74x152	

Series	Years	Comp.	Mass (g)	Size (mm)	THK (mm)
O50/1947N	1947	Paper		82x154	
O50/1953N	1953	Paper		97x169	
O50/1970N	1970	Paper		76x154	
O50/1977N	1977	Paper		76x154	
O50/1992N	1992	Paper		76x154	
O50/2002N	2002	Paper		77x140	

25.1. O50/1814N 1814 100 Gulden banknote (1814-1860)

Issued between 1814 and 1860. Although six slightly different versions were issued they all have hand written signatures. These notes looked like cheques and are printed in a large variety of font types and have an ornamental edge consisting of musical notes. They are printed in lilac on one side only.

Type	Signatures	P#	X
O50/1814Nyyyy	Several date and signature varieties.	A1, A6	

25.2. O50/1846N 1846 100 Gulden treasury note

Due to the introduction of the silver standard in 1850 large amounts of silver coins were necessary to exchange the gold coins that were no longer legal tender. As the production of large silver coins was not large enough paper money in the form of treasury notes were issued.

The note is printed on one side only and its colour is blue.

Type	Date	P#	X
O50/1846N	1 January 1846	A14	

25.3. O50/1849N 1849 100 Gulden treasury note

Issued after the former note lost its value. Printed on one side only. Printed in red/grey.

Type	Date	P#	X
O50/1849N	15 October 1849	A17	

25.4. O50/1853N 1853 100 gulden treasury note

Issued after the former note lost its value. As the notes now were used to finance the state debt they could not be withdrawn and were issued for a considerable time. This note is printed mostly in black.

Type	Date	P#	X
O50/1853N	15 September 1853		

25.5. O50/1860N 1860 100 Gulden banknote (1860-1921)

Printed on both sides with printed (no longer hand written) signatures.

Obverse: Minerva wearing helmet at top, "100" in all four corners. The note is printed in black.

Reverse: Printed in blue and black, large "100" in centre.

Type	Dates / Signatures	P#	X
O50/1860Nyyyy	Various dates between 1860 and 1921, six signature combinations.	24	

25.6. O40/1914N 1914 100 Gulden emergency banknote

Designed, printed and issued in a hurry due to fast disappearance of gold coins from circulation after the start of World War I. Apparently due to stabilisation of the situation this note was not circulated.

Obverse: Printed in black on rose, large "HONDERD GULDEN" in centre and ornamental edge.

Reverse: Not printed.

Type	Date	P#	X
O48/1914N	1 August 1914	32	

25.7. O50/1922N 1922 100 Gulden banknote (1922-1929)

During this period all higher value notes (100, 200, 300 and 1000 Gulden) had the same design. Due to a change in the text of the anti counterfeiting law two slightly different reverse versions have been issued.

Obverse A: Sitting woman at left. Printed in blue.

Reverse A[1]: Ornamental design with circles with large "100"s in the upper left and right corner. Penal code text starts with "Hij die bankbiljetten ..."

Reverse A[2]: As reverse A[1] but text of penal code starts with "Het namaken of ...".

Type	Dates / Signatures	P#	X
O50/1922NyyyyAA[1]	Various dates between 1922 and 1924, one signature combination.	41	
O50/1922NyyyyAA[2]	Various dates between 1926 and 1929, one signature combination.	41	

25.8. O50/1930N 1930 100 Gulden banknote (1930-1944)

Obverse   *Reverse*

Obverse: "100" in centre, at left and right top a woman's head. The colour is predominantly green.

Reverse: Ornamental design in centre with "100" in all four corners. The colour is green with lilac.

Type	Dates / Signatures	P#	X
O50/1930Nyyyy	Various dates between 1930 and 1944, four signature combinations.	49	

25.9. O50/1943N WWII 100 Gulden treasury note (1943)

Printed in the USA during World War II to be used as emergency money once the Netherlands would be liberated. Issued by the Treasury. Issued and circulated mostly in the liberated southern part of the country.

Obverse: Black. Portrait of Queen Wilhelmina in centre of note.

Reverse: Orange. Coat of arms of the Netherlands in centre of note.

Type	Date	P#	X
O50/1943N	4 February 1943	69	

25.10. O50/1945N 1945 100 Gulden banknote

Issued with one design and a fixed date.

Obverse: Ornamental design with "HONDERD GULDEN" in the centre. Printed in brown and lilac.

Reverse: "100"in centre. Mostly green.

Type	Date	P#	X
O50/1945N	7 May 1945	79	

25.11. O50/1947N 1947 100 Gulden banknote

Issued with one design and a fixed date.

Obverse: Portrait of woman at right. "100" at left. Printed in brown.

Reverse: Ornamental design, two large "100"s at lower left and right. Printed in green, blue and brown.

Type	Date	P#	X
O50/1947N	9 July 1947	82	

25.12. O50/1953N 1953 100 Gulden banknote

Issued with one design and a fixed date.

Obverse Portrait of the humanist Desiderius Erasmus (1466-1536) at right. Printed mostly in brown.

Reverse: Ornamental design with two large "100"s. Printed in brown and orange.

Type	Date	P#	X
O50/1953N	2 February 1953	85	

25.13. O50/1970N 1970 100 Gulden banknote

Issued with one design and a fixed date.

Obverse: Stylised portrait of the admiral Michiel de Ruyter (1607-1676) at right. Printed in brown.

Reverse: Stylised compass. Printed in brown.

Type	Date	P#	X
O50/1970N	14 May 1970	93	

25.14. O50/1977N 1977 100 Gulden banknote

Issued with one design and a fixed date.

Obverse   *Reverse*

Obverse: Snipe. Printed mostly in brown. Image from ECB website.

Reverse: Head of snipe. Printed in brown to yellow. Image from ECB website.

Type	Date	P#	X
O50/1977N	28 July 1977	97	

25.15. O50/1992N 1992 100 Gulden banknote

Issued with one design and a fixed date.

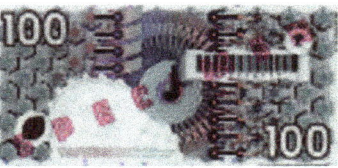

Obverse   *Reverse*

Obverse: Brown, abstract design representative of a little owl. Image from ECB website.

Reverse: Ornamental design, brown. Image from ECB website.

Type	Date	P#	X
O50/1992N	9 January 1992	101	

25.16. O50/2002N 1st series 50 Euro note (2002)

One design, three signature variations. Printed mostly in orange.

Obverse   *Reverse*

Obverse: Renaissance style architecture. Image from ECB website.

Reverse: Map of Europe with Renaissance style bridge. Image from ECB website.

Type	Signatures	P#	X
O50/2002Nyyyy	Duisenberg (2002), Trichet(2004), Draghi (2012)	4, 11, 17	

26. O53/ 200 Gulden (NLG 200.00); 100 Euro (EUR 100.00)

200 Gulden is issued as four banknote series between 1814 and 1927. 50 Euro is issued as one banknote series.

Series	Years	Comp.	Mass (g)	Size (mm)	THK (mm)
O53/1814N	1814-1860	Paper		Various	
O53/1860N	1860-1921	Paper		120x220	
O53/1914N	1914	Paper		130x210	
O53/1922N	1922-1927	Paper		122x215	
O53/2002N	2002	Paper		92x147	

26.1. O53/1814N 1814 200 Gulden note (1814-1860)

Issued between 1814 and 1860. Although six slightly different versions were issued they all have hand written signatures. These notes looked like cheques and are printed in a large variety of font types and have an ornamental edge consisting of musical notes. They are printed in lilac on one side only.

Type	Signatures	P#	X
O53/1814Nyyyy	Several date and signature varieties.	A1, A7	

26.2. O53/1860N 1860 200 Gulden note (1860-1921)

Printed on both sides. Signatures are printed.

Obverse: Woman wearing helmet (Minerva) at top, "200" in all four corners. The colour is black.

Reverse: Brown, large "200" in centre.

Type	Dates / Signatures	P#	X
O53/1860Nyyyy	Various dates between 1860 and 1921, five signature combinations.	25	

26.3. O53/1914N 1914 200 Gulden emergency banknote

Designed, printed and issued in a hurry due to fast disappearance of gold coins from circulation after the start of World War I. Apparently due to stabilisation of the situation this note was not circulated. Only one series of (10000) notes printed.

Obverse: Printed in black and orange, large "TWEE HONDERD GULDEN" in centre and ornamental edge.

Reverse: Not printed.

Type	Date	P#	X
O53/1914N	1 August 1914	32A	

26.4. O53/1922N 1922 200 Gulden banknote (1922-1927)

During this period all higher value notes (100, 200, 300 and 1000 Gulden) had the same design. Due to a change in the text of the anti counterfeiting law two slightly different reverse versions have been issued.

Obverse A: Sitting woman at left. The colour is red.

Reverse A[1]: Ornamental design with circles with large "300"s in the upper left and right corner. Penal code text starts with "Hij die bankbiljetten ..."

Reverse A[2]: As reverse A[1] but text of penal code starts with "Het namaken of ...".

Type	Dates / Signatures	P#	X
O50/1922NyyyyAA[1]	Various dates between 1922 and 1925, one signature combination.	42	
O50/1922NyyyyAA[2]	Various dates between 1926 and 1927, one signature combination.	42	

26.5. O53/2002N 1st series 100 Euro banknote (2002)

One design, three signature variations. Printed mostly in green.

Obverse　　　　　　　　*Reverse*

Obverse: Baroque and rococo style architecture. Image from ECB website.

Reverse: Map of Europe with baroque and rococo style bridge. Image from ECB website.

Type	Signatures	P#	X
O53/2002Nyyyy	Duisenberg (2002), Trichet (2004), Draghi (2012)	5, 12, 18	

27. O54/ 250 Gulden (NLG 250.00)

Only one banknote series was issued to fill the gap that existed between the 100 and 1000 Gulden banknotes during the 1980s.

Series	Years	Comp.	Mass (g)	Size (mm)	THK (mm)
O54/1985N	1985	Paper		76x160	

27.1. O54/1985N 1985 250 Gulden banknote

Issued with one design and a fixed date.

Obverse   *Reverse*

Obverse: Lighthouse, printed predominately in purple. Image from ECB website.

Reverse: Map representing the Netherlands coast. Image from ECB website.

Type	Date	P#	X
O54/1985N	25 July 1985	98	

28. O55/ 300 Gulden (NLG 300.00)

Issued as four banknote series between 1814 and 1927.

Series	Years	Comp.	Mass (g)	Size (mm)	THK (mm)
O55/1814N	1814-1859	Paper		Various	
O55/1860N	1860-1921	Paper		120x220	
O55/1914N	1914	Paper		130x210	
O55/1922N	1922-1927	Paper		122x215	

28.1. O55/1814N 1814 300 Gulden note (1814-1859)

Issued between 1814 and 1859. Although six slightly different versions were issued they all have hand written signatures. These notes looked like cheques and are printed in a large variety of font types and have an ornamental edge consisting of musical notes. They are printed in lilac on one side only.

Type	Signatures	P#	X
O55/1814Nyyyy	Several date and signature varieties.	A1, A8	

28.2. O55/1860N 1860 300 Gulden note (1860-1921)

Printed on both sides. Signatures are printed.

Obverse: Minerva wearing helmet at top, "300" in all four corners. The colour is black.

Reverse: Green, large "300" in centre.

Type	Dates / Signatures	P#	X
O55/1860Nyyyy	Various dates between 1860 and 1921, six signature combinations.	26	

28.3. O55/1914N 1914 300 Gulden emergency banknote

Designed, printed and issued in a hurry due to fast disappearance of gold coins from circulation after the start of World War I. Apparently due to stabilisation of the situation this note was not circulated. Only one series of (10000) notes printed.

Obverse: black and green, large "DRIE HONDERD GULDEN" in centre and ornamental edge.

Reverse: Not printed.

Type	Date	P#	X
O55/1914N	1 August 1914	32B	

28.4. O55/1922N 1922 300 Gulden banknote (1922-1927)

During this period all higher value notes (100, 200, 300 and 1000 Gulden) had the same design. Due to a change in the text of the anti counterfeiting law two slightly different reverse versions have been issued.

Obverse A: Sitting woman at left. The colour is green.

Reverse A^1: Ornamental design with circles with large "300"s in the upper left and right corner. Penal code text starts with "Hij die bankbiljetten ..."

Reverse A^2: As reverse A^1 but text of penal code starts with "Het namaken of ...".

Type	Dates / Signatures	P#	X
O55/1922NyyyyAA^1	Various dates in 1922 and 1925, one signature combination.	42	
O55/1922NyyyyAA^2	Various dates in 1926 and 1927, one signature combination.	42	

29. O56/ 200 Euro (EUR 200.00)

In circulation since 2002 after the introduction of the Euro as the new European currency. Only one note series has been produced since the introduction.

Series	Years	Comp.	Mass (g)	Size (mm)	THK (mm)
O56/2002N	2002	Paper		92x153	

29.1. O56/2002N 1st series 200 Euro banknote (2002)

One design, three signature variations. Printed mostly in yellow-brown.

Obverse   *Reverse*

Obverse: 19th century style architecture. Image from ECB website.

Reverse: Map of Europe with 19th century style steel bridge. Image from ECB website.

Type	Signatures	P#	X
O53/2002Nyyyy	Duisenberg (2002), Trichet(2004), Draghi (2012)	6, 13, 19	

30. O57/ 500 Gulden (NLG 500.00)

Issued as banknote in 1814 and 1930 and as treasury note in 1846 and 1849.

Series	Years	Comp.	Mass (g)	Size (mm)	THK (mm)
O57/1814N	1814-1836	Paper		Various	
O57/1846N	1846	Paper		85x167	
O57/1849N	1849	Paper		130x196	
O57/1930N	1930	Paper		128x220	

30.1. O57/1814N 1814 300 Gulden note (1814-1859)

Issued between 1814 and 1859. Although five slightly different versions were issued they all have hand written signatures. These notes looked like cheques and are printed in a large variety of font types and have an ornamental edge consisting of musical notes. They are printed in lilac on one side only.

Type	Signatures	P#	X
O57/1814Nyyyy	Several date and signature varieties.	A1, A9	

30.2. O57/1846N 1846 500 Gulden treasury note

Due to the introduction of the silver standard in 1850 large amounts of silver coins were necessary to exchange the gold coins that were no longer legal tender. As the production of large silver coins was not large enough paper money in the form of treasury notes were issued.

The note is printed on one side only and its colour is yellow.

Type	Date	P#	X
O57/1846N	1 January 1846	A15	

30.3. O57/1849N 1849 500 Gulden treasury note

Issued after the former note lost its value. Printed on one side only in brown and blue.

Type	Date	P#	X
O57/1849N	15 October 1849	A18	

30.4. O57/1930N 1930 500 Gulden banknote

Issued after the 300 Gulden bank note was no longer issued as denomination. As there was no large use for such a high denomination note (apart from the 1000 Gulden note) only a small number were issued.

Obverse: Head of Prince Willem III, the later king of England (1650-1702), with large ship below. Printed in blue.

Reverse: Ornamental design with two "500"s in the upper left and right corner.

Type	Signatures	P#	X
O57/1930Nyyyy	Several dates in 1930, one signature variety.	50	

31. O60/ 1000 Gulden (NLG 1000.00); 500 Euro (EUR 500.00)

In spite of the inflation that occurred, 1000 Gulden has always been the highest denomination that circulated in the Netherlands. The highest Euro denomination, 500 Euro is surprisingly close to 1000 Gulden and for that reason incorporated under the same heading. A total of eight 1000 Gulden banknote series and one treasury note series have been circulated. Until now one 500 Euro banknote series has circulated.

Series	Years	Comp.	Mass (g)	Size (mm)	THK (mm)
O60/1814N	1814-1859	Paper		Various	
O60/1849N	1849	Paper		130x196	
O60/1859N	1859-1921	Paper		120x220	
O60/1914N	1914	Paper		130x210	
O60/1919N	1919-1938	Paper		122x215	

Series	Years	Comp.	Mass (g)	Size (mm)	THK (mm)
O60/1945N	1945	Paper		85x150	
O60/1956N	1956	Paper		97x196	
O60/1972N	1972	Paper		76x160	
O60/1994N	1994	Paper		76x166	
O60/2002N	2002	Paper		82x160	

31.1. O60/1814N 1814 1000 Gulden banknote (1814-1859)

Issued between 1814 and 1859. Although six slightly different versions were issued they all have hand written signatures. These notes looked like cheques and are printed in a large variety of font types and have an ornamental edge consisting of musical notes. They are printed in lilac on one side only.

Type	Signatures	P#	X
O60/1814Nyyyy	Several date and signature varieties.	A1, A10	

31.2. O60/1849N 1849 1000 Gulden treasury note

Due to the introduction of the silver standard in 1850 large amounts of silver coins were necessary to exchange the gold coins that were no longer legal tender. As the production of large silver coins was not large enough paper money in the form of treasury notes were issued.

Type	Date	P#	X
O60/1849N	15 October 1849	A19	

31.3. O60/1859N 1859 1000 Gulden banknote (1860-1921)

Printed on both sides. Signatures are printed.

Obverse: Woman wearing helmet (Minerva) at top, "1000" in all four corners. The colour is black and blue.

Reverse: Red, large "1000" in centre.

Type	Dates / Signatures	P#	X
O60/1859Nyyyy	Various dates between 1859 and 1921, six signature combinations.	27	

31.4. O60/1914N O55/1914N 1914 1000 Gulden emergency banknote

Designed, printed and issued in a hurry due to fast disappearance of gold coins from circulation after the start of World War I. Only one series of (10000) notes printed.

Obverse: Much like O60/1859N but different font used and penal code on obverse. The colour is black and blue.

Reverse: Not printed.

Type	Date	P#	X
O55/1914N	1 August 1914	33	

31.5. O60/1919N 1919 1000 Gulden banknote (1919-1938)

During this period all higher value notes (100, 200, 300 and 1000 Gulden) had the same design. Two different colour series have been printed. Due to a change in the text of the anti counterfeiting law the text on the reverse has also been changed.

Obverse B   *Reverse B*

Obverse A: Sitting woman at left. Printed in black and brown.

Obverse B: As obverse A but printed in green and lilac.

Reverse A: Ornamental design with circles with large "1000"s in the upper left and right corner. Printed in brown. Penal code text starts with "Hij die bankbiljetten ...".

Reverse B: As reverse A but now printed in brown, red and green. Penal code text starts with "Het namaken of ...".

Type	Dates / Signatures	P#	X
O55/1922NyyyyAA	Various dates in 1919 and 1920, one signature combination.	44	
O55/1922NyyyyBB	Various dates between 1926 and 1938, three signature combinations.	45	

31.6. O60/1945N 1945 1000 Gulden banknote

Issued with one design and a fixed date.

Obverse: Prince Willem I (the Silent, 1533-1584) at right. Printed in gray, green and orange.

Reverse: The "Afsluitdijk" (Dam that closes the IJsselmeer from the sea). Printed mostly in blue.

Type	Date	P#	X
O60/1945N	7 May 1945	80	

31.7. O60/1956N 1956 1000 Gulden banknote

Issued in one design with a fixed date.

Obverse: Portrait of the painter Rembrandt van Rijn

(1606-1669) at right. Printed in green and red.

Reverse: Hand painting, printed in green.

Type	Date	P#	X
O60/1956N	15 July 1956	89	

31.8. O60/1972N 1972 1000 Gulden banknote

Issued in one design with a fixed date.

Obverse   *Reverse*

Obverse: Stylised portrait of the philosopher Baruch Spinoza (1632-1677) at right. Printed in green. Image from ECB website.

Reverse: Ornamental pattern. Printed in green. Image from ECB website.

Type	Date	P#	X
O60/1972N	30 March 1972	94	

31.9. O60/1994N 1994 1000 Gulden banknote

Issued in one design with a fixed date.

Obverse   *Reverse*

Obverse: Green, abstract design representative of a pewit. Image from ECB website.

Reverse: Ornamental design, green. Image from ECB website.

Type	Date	P#	X
O60/1994N	2 June 1994	103	

31.10. O60/2002N 1ˢᵗ series 500 Euro banknote (2002)

One design, three signature variations. Printed mostly in purple.

Obverse   *Reverse*

Obverse: Modern 20ᵗʰ century style architecture. Image from ECB website.

Reverse: Map of Europe with Modern 20ᵗʰ century style bridge. Image from ECB website.

Type	Signatures	P#	X
O60/2002Nyyyy	Duisenberg (2002), Trichet(2004), Draghi (2012)	7, 14, 20	

Literature

Akkermans, C. and Vercoulen, P. (2006) Catalogus van HET NEDERLANDSE PAPIERGELD 1814 – 2006. 2ⁿᵈ edition.

Bonneville, A. (1849) Encyclopédie Monétaire ou Nouveau Traité des Monnaies d'Or et d'Argent en circulation chez les diverse peuples du monde. Available from Google Books, https://books.google.nl/books?id=rz9JAAAAcAAJ.

CIA (2014) The World Factbook; The Netherlands;

available at: https://www.cia.gov/library/publications/the-world-factbook/geos/nl.html [accessed 14th November 2014]

European Central Bank (2016) http://www.ecb.europa.eu/euro/banknotes/html/index.en.html (information) and http://www.ecb.europa.eu/euro/shared/img/euro_banknotes_specimen_72dpi.zip?0fd56ed419aedf5d2d53d2fd668ddc12 (Downloadable banknote images) [accessed 6th January 2016].

Imprensa Nacional Casa de Moeda (2015) The euro circulations coins: https://www.incm.pt/portal/mpm_euro.jsp?lang=en [this URL contains information on the mass of the cores of the 1 and 2 Euro coins, accessed 7th February 2015]

Instituut voor Monetaire Geschiedenis en Numismatiek (2012) De Nederlandse Muntwetgeving 1813-2002; available at: http://www.simgn.nl/PUBLICATIES/WETTEN/_WETTEN.html [accessed 4th November 2014]

Krause, C.L. and Mishler, C. (1998) 1999 standard catalog of World coins. 26th edition. Krause Publications, Inc, Iola, WI.

Krause, C.L. and Mishler, C. (1999) Standard catalog of World coins. 1801-1900. Second edition. Krause Publications, Inc, Iola, WI.

Kraut, J.C. and Stern, W.B. (2000) The density of gold-silver-copper alloys and its calculation from the chemical composition. Gold Bulletin, 33(2), 52-55.

Mevius, J. (1997) Speciale catalogus van de Nederlandse munten van 1795 tot heden. Mevius Numisbooks Int. B.V., Vriezenveen.

Mevius, J. and Lelivelt, F.G. (1981) De Nederlandse bankbiljetten van 1814 tot heden. Tweede editie. Mevius

Numisbooks Int. B.V., Vriezenveen.

Nederlandse Vereniging van Munthandelaren (2009) Muntalmanak 2010. Uitg. De Vleermuis, Roermond.

Pick, A. (1980) Standard Catalog of World Paper Money. 3rd edition. Krause Publishers.

Plomp, P. (2015) Catalogus Nederlands Papiergeld 1573-2002. 1st Edition.

Schön, G and Kahn, H. (2014) Weltmünzkatalog 19. Jahrhundert. Battenberg verlag.

Schön, G and Schön, G. (2014) Welmunzkatalog 20. & 21. Jahrhundert. 42. Aulage. Battenberg Verlag.

Schulman, J. (1975) Handboek van de Nederlandse munten van 1795 tot 1975. 5de geheel herziene en verbeterde druk. Jacques Schulman B.V., Amsterdam.

Shafer, N. and Cuhaj, G.S. (2003) Standard catalog of world paper money. Volume three. Modern issues 1961-date. Krause Publications Inc, Iola, WI.

Van Gelder, E. (2002) De Nederlandse munten. Het complete overzicht tot en met de komst van de euro. 8ste herziene en aangevulde druk. Uitg. Het Spectrum B.V., Utrecht

Verkade, P. (1848) Muntboek bevattende de namen en afbeeldingen van munten geslagen in de zeven voormalig Vereenigde Nederlandsche Provincien sedert de vrede van Gent tot op onzen tijd. P.J. van Dijk, Schiedam. Available from Google Books; https://books.google.nl/books?id=RGU-AQAAMAAJ.

Yeoman, R.S. (2008) A catalog of modern World coins 1850-1964. 14th edition. Whitman Publishing LLC, Atlanta GA.